THE
21 DAY
BLAST
PLAN

Lose inches, gain strength
and reboot your body

ANNIE DEADMAN

HQ
An imprint of HarperCollins*Publishers* Ltd
1 London Bridge Street
London SE1 9GF

10 9 8 7 6 5 4 3 2 1

First published in Great Britain by HQ
An imprint of HarperCollins*Publishers* Ltd 2018

ISBN 978-0-00- 825925-9

Photography: Andrew Burton
Food styling: Emily Jonzen
Prop styling: Olivia Wardle
Design & Art Direction: Hart Studio
Editorial Director: Rachel Kenny
Project Editor: Sarah Hammond
Creative Director: Louise McGrory

Printed and bound at GPS Group

I'd like to dedicate this book to all the brilliant
people around the world who have Blast-ed
their way to a better understanding of nutrition,
a fervent love of squats and a body they're proud of

CONTENTS

Breakfasts & Brunches
Light Meals, Soups & Salads
Hearty Meals
Sides, Dips & Relishes
Snacks

PART 3
THE WORKOUTS:
Getting fit, firm & strong . . . and maybe a bit sweaty

PART 4
FILLING IN THE GAPS:
Knowledge is power

HELLO

My name is Annie Deadman and I'm the extremely proud creator of The 21 Day Blast plan, a three-week healthy-eating and fitness programme that, in a nutshell, kicks your sweet tooth into touch, calms your gut and leaves you with less fat and firmer muscles.

Just so you know, I'm not some fake who went 'on a diet' once, found it worked and decided to flog it the masses. I have for the last fifteen years or so been running Annie Deadman Training, which provides fitness-training sessions, personal training and Pilates courses to the local community in southwest London.

I am in my fifties, have two gorgeous daughters in their twenties, a team of bossy instructors and a studio where people come and go all day long, for personal training sessions.

As a child, I was chubby. As a teenager, chubby turned into overweight with a dash of geeky and shy – the future in terms of mixing with the opposite sex wasn't looking bright. So I ditched the short skirts, flexed what little muscle I had and threw myself into schoolwork. PE, it turned out, wasn't one of my favourites and I, like most of the other self-conscious girls, skived off as often as I could.

At university, everyone around me seemed to be on a diet of fags . . . or just on a diet. Inevitably I joined in. I turned to starvation as a means of losing weight and life became all bran flakes and cottage cheese. I was hungry all the time and I never once thought about my health or, heaven forbid, about exercise. I emerged from university, found a job in London and yo-yo dieted my way through the next five years.

It was only when I got married and had my first child at the age of thirty-two that things changed again. High interest rates, two recessions and a colossal mortgage meant my husband and I worked long and different hours and hardly ever ate together. As if the whole full-time working-mother thing wasn't enough, I was also facing something very like single parenthood and it started to leave its mark on my body. What had been an average OK-ish figure was now punctuated by wodges of unbecoming fat. My self-esteem plummeted at the same rate as my waistline expanded. I was in my early thirties but I felt dumpy and frumpy. Something had to be done.

After a particularly sticky weight-related conversation with my GP one day, I gave myself a talking-to and decided that I couldn't put it off any longer. I had to do some exercise. As an exercise virgin, the obvious first step was running. So off I went . . . not very far. Or very fast! But it was hideous. I got hot and it hurt and I felt uncomfortable. My second bite of the exercise cherry was more successful when I joined a local conditioning class and I started to use my muscles in a controlled way. It was actually rather pleasant, which meant I stuck to it, and very soon I started to see results. I firmed up and gained strength, and in the process, doubled my energy levels. Getting into shape didn't mean running endless miles. I was so happy to find that out.

This investment of effort also meant I started to be much more interested in eating good, nutritious meals. Less picking, more planning. Less beige, more green. Less emphasis on the pick-me-up chocolate and wine, more focus on cooking quick but healthy meals. I felt different, better.

My interest in health and body nourishment gathered pace and I enrolled on a part-time nutrition course at St Mary's University,

Twickenham. I devoured books on gut health and weight loss and started to realise that this was more than just a mild interest: I wanted desperately to share it with others.

A downsize house move meant I could swap to part-time work and so I started to study in my spare time to become a personal trainer. I turned the dilapidated old garage into a studio and bribed the children to help me deliver leaflets door to door. This heralded the start of Annie Deadman Training. I wanted to encourage and motivate. My passion to help others find their groove and my 'tell it how it is' approach meant that word got out and soon my days were filled with clients. I was helping men and women to feel better (inside and out), to get stronger and to embrace their lives with refreshed confidence. A steady expansion in the next few years meant I took on a small team of trainers and I was able to offer a whole range of group fitness-training sessions to the local community

I learnt so much (and continue to) from all my clients about their day-to-day issues, their food intolerances, their lack of time. There was a pattern emerging: men and women struggling to keep in shape (as well as hold on to some modicum of self-esteem) while managing a family and work, dishing up healthy meals and trying occasionally to come up for air. Bad habits had become entrenched and they just couldn't shake them off.

Personal training is, in the grand scheme of things, expensive and I wanted to find a way of helping people get into shape without having to join a gym or feeling constrained financially. I wanted to give them access to something that could help them break habits but not the bank. A short-term plan for fat loss and fitness with long-term results that was sustainable alongside the responsibilities of work and family.

I wanted to educate, motivate and entertain.

So the 21 Day Blast was born, an online fat-loss plan available to everyone around the world, offering an eating plan, recipes and workouts. Very soon after, Blast received some fantastic coverage in the national press and – bang! – overnight a wonderful Blast community was created.

Now I'm bringing the Blast plan to you within the covers of this book, so that you too can benefit from all that Blast offers, for 21 days and beyond. You're in for such a fun time. Let's get stuck in.

INTRODUCTION

The 21 Day Blast plan is a fat-loss and fitness plan. It's a programme of short workouts, which can easily be squeezed into anyone's week (at a time best for you), and a way of eating that means the body isn't wasting its effort dealing with digestive problems or storing fat. It is going to use the fat as fuel! And you are going to get fitter and stronger in the process.

'What? In 21 days? . . . Oh come on'

Yes, not long, is it? But during that time you will experience a way of eating and a way of exercising that you can (and will want to) continue on your own. You will learn which systems in the body work with you and which work against you and just how brimming with energy you can be.

In short, this is a self-help manual of empowerment, full of deadly serious facts with more than a sprinkling of humour.

'I've only just about enough energy to sort my family out, let alone dabble with empowerment . . .'

Hear me out.

You might be coming towards the end of your thirties and are juggling work, commutes, sleepless children and parents' evenings. You feel ongoing pressure to prepare nutritious, tasty home-cooked fodder (big on kale, low on pizza). You strive to be outstanding at work, the pinnacle of parenthood and manage a sparkling social life, despite a nagging desire to run amok with a bottle of Pinot Grigio and let it all descend into chaos.

Or you're trying desperately to withstand the test of time as your body heads for middle age or even the menopause, while being the best possible mother, friend, wife and lover, all with one eye on a waistline that has slid into your hips and another on the clock wondering if your teenage children are home yet.

As our years advance (fingers in ears . . . la-la-la-la), we can tuck all kinds of experience (and back fat) under our arms. Marriage, children, divorce, debilitating illnesses, the loss of parents . . . stuff that life throws at us. Big stuff that we have to deal with and emerge from looking sensible and grown-up. Consequently our health and our own efforts at staying in shape fall to the bottom of the list.

I've been through it all and more and I know the 21 Day Blast plan will help you get a tighter hold on everything.

'Annie Deadman, I am so done with diets; nothing works'

The 21 Day Blast plan is not a diet. It's a programme of better eating and exercise, during which you will deal with sugar and carbohydrate cravings. You will be eating in a way that's going to soothe your gut, boost your energy levels and subsequently your mood. You will be using food to help you burn fat and create a body that is harmonious, inside as well as out. Twenty-one days is enough time to break well-entrenched habits. We're talking that wind-down wine at the end of every day and the TV chocolate.

Yes, we all love those things. And no, it doesn't mean you won't ever have them again. It just means that over these 21 days you will find out what highs and lows certain foods bring to your mood, your sleep and most of all the bits on your body that are surplus to requirements.

'So you're going to help me take control? Lose fat and get into shape?'

Dead right I am. And that's just in 21 days.

This book is a super-easy read. There are some food guidelines and principles to follow and some workouts to do during each of the three weeks. If you eat like this and do the workouts you will lose fat.

'Tell me I don't have to spend hours in the gym when I should be waving the homework stick and force-feeding my children broccoli'

No, you don't. The workouts are between twenty and thirty minutes long and you need no equipment. And as for the food, it's all normal – it's just a matter of swapping a few things around.

This book is going to show you how to get serious with yourself and take charge. You'll become slimmer and fitter. You'll discover new routines and you'll be motivated enough to sustain them. This is a bold statement, but I'd really like this to be the last book about losing fat that you ever, ever pick up.

So, if you fancy a good shot at losing a few inches, taking control, kicking your sweet tooth into touch, feeling downright gorgeous and having a bit of a giggle along the way, then let's get on with it.

Remember one thing: I'm on your side.

'Six months ago I was bursting out of my clothes and needed to buy a size 16. This was the turning point for me. I had never been "big" and here I was, FAT! Three Blast programmes later and I am a size 12. I focus on size and the tape measure and overall I have lost a total of 17 inches. SEVENTEEN!!! Needless to say I am delighted. Thank you so much.'

J.P., London

HOW TO GET THE MOST OUT OF THIS BOOK

Here, I've laid out a plan of all the chapters in this book so you can see at a glance what's in store.

But before we go any further, I just want to say something. No one ever lost fat (and sustained it), increased their energy levels and had a happy body and mind by chewing lettuce and sitting still. Very low-calorie diet plans make us miserable because they leave us thinking incessantly about food. There is NOTHING more destructive to one's weight-loss plans than being constantly hungry.

So we're going to be doing plenty of eating . . . and some exercising. Both of those things. Any successful fat-loss plan involves focus on both the nutrition side of things as well as exercise. It's actually getting going and making that first move that is the hard part, but we're in this together, so let's crack on and let me tell you how this Blast manual is going to help you not only lose fat and inches but also get fitter and stronger – inside as well as out.

Firstly, this is how the book is structured.

PART 1: FOOD & OUR BODIES
The background to Blast fat loss

'How come that woman on Instagram can stuff her face with tacos and soured cream but her thighs are the same size as my arms and I'm sitting here with a crispbread and cottage cheese?'

Galling, isn't it?

In these chapters we grasp the concepts of why and how we put on fat and we look at the part our hormones play and how their groove can upset our groove. We'll also take a good, close look at the food groups and see how they can both help and hinder our fat-loss efforts.

It's four glorious chapters of entertainment but deadly serious facts. Let's call it preparation.

PART 2: THE BLAST EATING PLAN & RECIPES
The food, the rules, the tools

'They devoured the meals with relish and never even noticed I was following a fitness programmme. And my husband lost weight too . . . he wasn't hungry once! Thank you so much, Annie, this has really changed our lives.'

V.W., Derby

This is the nub of the book and the section that equips you for success. It tells you exactly how you're going to be eating for 21 days, how you will focus less on sugary foods that soothe your emotions and more on the right food to fuel your body, soothe your gut and bring power to your muscles.

It's packed with really delicious, inspirational cooking ideas, not just to fuel you through the day but to satisfy your heart and your head too. You don't have to be a gourmet chef (if only . . .) and you'll have most ingredients already in your store cupboard. There are full-blown recipes as well as simple meal suggestions, which involve more assembling than creating, for busier days.

The Blast guidelines adapt perfectly to everyday family eating, so you won't find yourself confronted by a plate of diet-y food, while the rest of the family tucks in to something different. Yes, there will be changes to make and change means effort, newness, unfamiliarity. But it also means swap around, improve, revamp, convert. That's all we're doing.

The third part of this section is given over to positive strategy advice as well as practical tips on how to gauge your fat-loss progress – seeing your results will become your motivation.

PART 3: THE WORKOUT SECTION

Getting fit, firm & strong . . . and maybe a bit sweaty

'What a fantastic plan. I loved (and hated) the workouts. By week 3, I was getting an endorphin rush after the exercise and finding it a great de-stress after a hard day at work.'
K.H., London

I can hear you inwardly groan. It won't go away. Yes, you could tear the pages out and pretend they weren't there but you'd be chucking out half the fat-loss equation. These workouts are the vital factor in accelerating and sustaining your results.

I'll say that word again . . . sustaining. Not for a week, not for Christmas, not for 21 days. For always.

Check out the different levels, decide which is yours and then follow those workouts, using the pictures and instructions to help you.

Towards the end of the section there's advice for those who want to go above and beyond the Blast call of duty and do extra workouts, plus helpful motivation in maintaining a workout habit after the 21 days are finished.

PART 4: FILLING IN THE GAPS
Knowledge is power!

> 'I have totally changed the way
> I eat now . . . I can still have
> treats, but they're no longer
> a daily crutch. Thank you
> so much.'
>
> G.P., Shropshire

This section is devoted to helping you make informed decisions about what's worth listening to and what isn't. I talk about intermittent fasting and its benefits and how you can incorporate it into the 21 Day Blast plan, if you choose. Well-known myths are given the once-over and I tackle common fat-loss questions.

There's also a special section towards the end. This is a great place to come for a 'tell it how it is' dose of motivation. Days 1 to 21 are little paragraphs of fun for you to read as you work your way through the 21 Day Blast plan. They're similar to the daily email I write to all who take part in the online version of the Blast plan. They will help to keep you on track and fired up.

The section ends with a chapter about life after Blast. During the Blast plan you are going to experience some new eating habits. This chapter offers helpful guidance on how to continue to lose fat while adapting those habits to your daily life for ever.

'So, Annie Deadman, what do I get for investing in this book and handing my body and soul over to you?'

Oh, goody. I was hoping you'd ask that. Gives me the chance for one of my lists. Here are the benefits of Blast, in all their glory.

- You will lose fat and therefore inches
- You will have stronger, firmer muscles and better tone
- Your sweet tooth won't know what to do with itself
- Your gut will be calm – less gurgling, wind and bloating
- Symptoms of eczema, hay fever and mucus congestion will lessen
- Your fitness will increase, which means your heart can push more blood around the body with fewer pumps . . . win, win!
- We are at the mercy of our hormones and Blast helps regulate them and their more negative effects
- Your sleep will be deeper and your skin will shine
- Habits you thought you would never crack will become old crutches of the past
- You will be firing on all cylinders – you will have boundless energy
- You will be giving your body the greatest chance of staying in the best possible shape and health

So, lovely people, shall we find out what Blast is all about?

1

FOOD & OUR BODIES

THE BACKGROUND TO BLAST FAT LOSS

Chapter 1

A CLOSER LOOK AT FOOD GROUPS

(or . . . if we want to be posh . . . the macronutrients and micronutrients)

Recently, I met up with an old friend who had some outpouring to do. We hadn't seen each other for a while and we were chewing the fat (pun intended) over a bottle of Chardonnay. By the second glass the floodgates had opened and we were on the sticky subject of her weight gain.

'Look at me, Annie, what's happened? I hate myself. Years ago I could at least run for the train and not pass out. I knew the importance of green veg and I slid into a size 14 like a dream. I wore lipstick every day and I strutted my stuff up and down the office. I knew how to fight my corner and I enjoyed life. Now I'm a size 18 . . . on a good day . . . and I wobble when I walk, let alone run. My trousers dig in, my thighs chafe, my feet are always swollen and I'm hot with a damp top lip all day. I buy outsize clothes and I eat outsize meals but I haven't been hungry since 2004. Bar amputation I have no idea how to get this weight off.'

She and I, we go way back, so I allowed myself to hoot with laughter. But deep down, I knew my lovely friend was begging to peel back the years and the layers to find her old self again.

Before any of us can do that, we need to understand how important food is when trying to lose fat. No, not necessarily eating less, just eating better.

'I can feel a double biology lesson coming on . . .'

Yes, but much more fun. Stick with me.

Stand in front of the mirror. Starkers. Go on. Now, when no one's looking, grab hold of a handful of the spare flesh that lies in places you don't like.

We're going to take a brief look at how that got there, how it's affecting your health, your personal harmony, wellbeing and happiness, and how we can get rid of it. By and large, it gets there through the stuff you put into your mouth, and how your body reacts to it. You may even discover that you have a slight intolerance to the foods you've been eating all these years and maybe that has held you back from achieving what you want. The 21 Day Blast plan will give you the tools to make discoveries about not only your own fat-losing potential but also other minor health issues. One woman who took part in a 21 Day Blast plan in early spring was shocked to find that her hay-fever symptoms totally disappeared during the 21-day period.

So, this next bit is the background knowledge you'll need. It will cement your understanding of why Blast is going to help you lose fat.

In order to stay alive and function properly, our bodies need nutrients. If we're being pernickety, the true meaning of nutrient is 'a substance that provides nourishment essential for the maintenance of life and for growth'.

Macronutrients make up the bulk of our food. We need big quantities of these and they can be divided up into **carbohydrates**, **proteins** and **fats**. Alcohol is also classed as a macronutrient but doesn't actually provide any life-giving nutrition. I know . . . shame.

Micronutrients come in the shape of vitamins and minerals and we only need small amounts of these. They will be present in a whole range of natural foods. They are not present in processed foods and they are vital for completing the healthy picture. They are the icing on our cake . . . or rather the broccoli on our steak and chips. Let's take a closer look at both these groups.

THE MACRONUTRIENTS

CARBOHYDRATE

Everyone flinches when you mention carbohydrates.

They're not bad for you. They're the petrol in your tank and they give us energy to move and think. Don't let anyone tell you otherwise. Good natural carbohydrate-rich foods are absolutely vital for our muscles, for energy and for our brain function. They are also essential for our digestive systems. They have received bad press because if we eat too much carb-rich food but don't actually move that much, then the body stores the surplus as fat.

Carbohydrate covers a whole range of foods: fruit, vegetables, oats, pasta, rice, potatoes, sugar. And then there's processed sugary foods such as cakes, biscuits, buns, chocolate – which I sometimes refer to as drug food – impossible to stop at one!

They are ALL carbohydrates and so they tend to be tarred with the same brush because they are the first food group to be modified in any fat-loss plan. Which is why their reputation in the media has gone from bad to worse.

We at Blast HQ like carbohydrates. A lot. But we like them at the right time. And we like them to be the right sort. The more natural the food, the more vitamins and minerals they will contain, and the better they are for our health, our wellbeing and our body shape.

'Yawn. Heard it all before. Got to do the whole green, wholefood, wholegrain thing . . . How come those lovely little chocolate biscuit thingies I enjoy each evening don't do the same job? They're carbs, too, aren't they?'

They are. Read on.

Complex carbohydrates from natural sources (oats, potatoes, brown rice) will be converted much more slowly into usable energy (glucose) than simple carbohydrates (sugary products, some fruits, your chocolate thingies). The more processed and sugary the food is, the quicker it will be converted into glucose.

So there you are on the sofa nibbling your family bag of chocolate things creating lots of glucose. But you have no intention of using up that glucose (you're still on the sofa), so the body has to do something with it.

Yes.

It drives that glucose into the fat cells and locks it up. And what's worse, it takes a lot of effort for those fat cells to give it up, unless we make some small changes to the way we eat. I talk much more in the next chapter about what happens to that glucose in those fat cells, but for now, let's have a look at another food group: protein.

PROTEIN

Protein is pretty top dog, in terms of the food on our plate. Every cell in the human body contains protein, so that gives you some idea of how important it is. We need protein not only to build and repair these cells but also (I can feel a list coming on, stay awake) . . .

- For the making of enzymes and chemical reactions in the body (stuff that happens without us noticing)

- In muscle contraction (you're going to need to do a bit of that)

- In the manufacture of hormones, which send messages around the body

- To make haemoglobin, which carries oxygen around the body

- The repair and strengthening of bones, hair and nails

Protein is made up of building blocks called amino acids, of which there are twenty different types. Twelve of them can be made in the body but the other eight must come from our food. Meat, fish and eggs are known as 'complete proteins' because they provide all twenty of the amino acids.

Nodded off yet?

The eight amino acids that we must get from our food are known as 'essential amino acids'. It's an odd term since they are no less important than the other twelve. They are – brace yourself – leucine, lysine, isoleucine, phenylalanine, methionine, tryptophan, threonine and valine.

The best sources of these eight essential amino acids are animal products. However, if you're a vegetarian who eats eggs and dairy, then you will manage to obtain all of them. If you're vegan and opting for a more plant-based way of eating, then you should focus on foods that contain high levels of lysine. That's because foods that contain even very small amounts of lysine will also contain substantial amounts of the other essential amino acids, so you will be sure to get enough of the whole package. Examples of lysine-rich foods are tofu and tempeh (also a soya product but more flavourful than tofu). Pistachio nuts, black beans, quinoa, soya milk and pumpkin seeds are also good sources.

Protein repairs our muscle tissue. During the 21 Day Blast plan you will be doing some exercise, and during that exercise your muscles will be challenged and placed under stress, but in a good way. Ensuring that you have enough protein in your meals will help the muscles repair, recover and keep them strong and firm. This also means that the body's systems are more likely to use your body fat for fuel rather than to start breaking down this muscle. Holding on to our muscle is vital for successful fat loss and I will be droning on about this in Chapter 9. To aid protein awareness, so to speak, I've added the grams of protein per portion to each recipe in Chapter 8.

Now, on to fat. That's dietary fat, not the stuff round our middle.

FAT

Fat is absolutely essential in your diet. Don't let any book, newspaper, magazine, bloke down the pub fob you off with some story about fat being fattening. Yes, it's high in calories (9 calories per gram, compared to protein and carbohydrates, which are both 4 calories) and that's probably where the reputation has come from. So you only need a little dose to give your health and weight-loss processes a massive leg-up.

So why is fat important?

- It is vital in the production of those hormones

- It provides you with energy

- Fat makes your food taste delicious

- Every cell in the body has a layer of fat, so fat is essential to keep these cells healthy

- Fat cushions and protects your organs and nerves

- It is a powerful aid in the absorption of fat-soluble vitamins (A, D, E and K . . . that's eyesight, bones, skin, immune system and heart-disease prevention, in a nutshell)

This next bit is worth learning off by heart – and reciting to anyone who will listen . . .

Back in the day, fat was hailed as a major contributor towards heart disease, strokes and a challenge to good health. We were sucked in and we believed it. This led to a whopping rise . . . and rise . . . of the 'LOW FAT' label.

The fat was taken out of food products and sugar was added in its place. This meant it was cheap and its shelf life was long.

'Yesssss . . .' thought the food manufacturers, thumping the boardroom table. 'Result!'

Alas, it was us, the consumer, who lost out. The added sugar made them moreish. Too moreish. Addictive even. If you dump this book and read no further, make a promise to yourself that you'll scrutinise a few labels on your next food-shopping trip. You'll see what I mean.

Nearly done with fat. We just need to gen up on the different types. Couple of matchsticks for your eyelids for this next bit.

- Saturated fats (meat, eggs, dairy, coconut oil): Saturated fat's previous bad reputation for being a main player in the causes of heart disease, strokes and other inflammatory conditions has eased. It's a natural product and has a rightful place in our diet.

- Unsaturated fats: These can be categorised into monounsaturated (avocados, nuts, seeds, some oils, like rapeseed, groundnut and olive oil) and polyunsaturated (vegetable oils and oily fish), which comes in two forms, omega-6 and omega-3. Omega-3 can't be made by the body, so that means we need to make sure we eat it. Oily fish such as salmon and mackerel are great sources, but if they turn your stomach then a variety of nuts and seeds will make sure you are filling that fat gap.

- Transfats: Sometimes known as hydrogenated fats, or trans-fatty acids, these fats started out life as polyunsaturated liquid fats and have been chemically processed with the addition of hydrogen. Shall I repeat those words?

Chemically processed.

This makes them into hydrogenated fats and their molecules change shape. They have morphed into something unrecognisable.

Despite this, food manufacturers love them and they make regular appearances in processed fast foods, such as biscuits, cakes, pies and pizza.

Transfats have no known nutritional benefits and research shows that they increase blood cholesterol levels (the bad stuff) and the risk of heart disease.

On Blast we don't cut out food groups. But for this little mini sub-group, we do. Transfats are not on the Blast menu.

'Oh Lord. You're going to say the words "clean eating" aren't you?'

No, as it happens I'm not. But I AM going to say this. I promised I would show you how to lose body fat and a way of eating that will soothe your insides and highlight any intolerances that may have been preventing you from losing fat in the past. This means the food you will be eating will cause the minimum of disruption to your digestive system. I'm not an advocate of the 'if you can't pick it or kill then don't eat it' rule, but I absolutely am all for fuelling our bodies with good, delicious unprocessed fare that is easy to cook, delicious to eat and will put a spring in your step.

The 21 Day Blast plan will trim and shape. It will empower the faint-hearted, firm the slack, reignite the flagging and make you strut your stuff like a goddess.

I am NOT, repeat NOT, going to make you become a slave to kale.

ALCOHOL

Yes, it's a food group. And, yes, we feel warm, fluffy and invincible when we've filled our boots with fizz. Sadly, it does nothing to help us in our weight loss. Head over to Chapter 3 where I give it the full treatment.

Moving on . . .

'Being over 50, I've seen improvements in the last 10 days that no expensive creams or even Botox could achieve.'

C.F., Surrey

THE MICRONUTRIENTS

In short, these are what are known as vitamins and minerals. Vitamins and minerals are the bees' knees for our normal growth, for our health and for bodily functions. We can't make them in the body, so we have to get them from our food, but we only need very small amounts.

'Is that it? Nothing else?'

Oh, yes. One more thing. Your health could degenerate if you don't get enough of these vits and mins. You'll never know if you're not getting enough (unless you cough up lots of money to go and see a specialist), but the best way to ensure you are giving yourself and your body the best possible chance is to eat a varied diet with heaps of vegetables of all different colours.

Oh, go on then, twist me arm . . . here's another of our lists.

I've selected the most important vitamins and minerals. These are the ones you should aim to be consuming every day. You probably will be, without realising it. Please don't become paranoid – this is intended as a simple guide. But do try and develop a love of broccoli . . . just saying . . .

VITAMIN A

What it does: Helps growth and repair of bones, skin, teeth and eyes as well as supporting our immune system.

Good food sources: Eggs, oily fish, liver, yoghurt, butternut squash, yellow and red peppers, tomatoes, carrots, sweet potatoes and yellow fruits, like mango, papaya, apricots.

VITAMIN B6

What it does: Helps the nervous and immune systems function well, assists in the production of some hormones and helps the body gain energy from food.

Good food sources: Fish, pork, chicken, turkey, starchy vegetables, oats, chickpeas, rice, tofu, spinach and other leafy greens.

VITAMIN B12

What it does: Helps in the making of red blood cells, in the releasing of energy from food and in our use of folic acid, preventing anaemia.

Good food sources: Meat, salmon, milk, cod, eggs. Vegans should take fortified soya milk, use nutritional yeast in their cooking or take a supplement to ensure their levels are topped up. Spirulina is an alga that comes in powder form and is regularly hailed as a superfood (we're talking high in protein as well as many vitamins and minerals). Add it to your shakes or mix it with water, hold your nose and neck it back like a shot. Its worthiness may help you forget its not especially lovely taste.

VITAMIN C

What it does: An antioxidant that will protect skin, blood vessels, bones and help with wound healing, as well as protect against infections.

Good food sources: Broccoli, red and green peppers, Brussels sprouts, strawberries, blackcurrants and potatoes.

CALCIUM

What it does: Essential for bone health, regulates muscle contractions and aids normal blood clotting.

Good food sources: Broccoli, cabbage, spinach, kale, sesame seeds, dairy products, tofu, soya beans and sardines (as long as you eat the bones too).

VITAMIN D

What it does: Enhances calcium absorption to keep bones and teeth strong. A vitamin D deficiency can lead to osteoporosis and has been linked to certain cancers, as well as to multiple sclerosis, type-1 diabetes and other chronic illnesses.

Good food sources: Oily fish, red meat, eggs, soya milk, tofu and mushrooms. The body also produces its own vitamin D when exposed to sunlight (20 minutes without sunscreen three times a week minimum).

VITAMIN E

What it does: Helps maintain healthy skin and eyes and upholds our immune system.

Good food sources: Almonds, avocados, vegetable oil (such as safflower and sunflower), sunflower seeds, spinach.

IRON

What it does: Iron is important in the manufacture of red blood cells, which transport oxygen round the body.

Good food sources: Red meat, dark green veg (oh, that must mean broccoli), beans, nuts, seeds and whole-grains, such as brown rice.

IODINE

What it does: Helps the thyroid gland produce thyroxine to stimulate and regulate metabolism.

Good food sources: Seafood, all seaweed, such as nori, wakame and kelp, potatoes, bananas, cranberries and strawberries.

VITAMIN K

What it does: Helps maintain healthy blood clotting and promotes bone density and strength by helping vitamin D do its job.

Good food sources: Kale, cabbage, Brussels sprouts, broccoli and vegetable oils, such as olive and soybean.

FLUIDS

We've covered the food groups and those vital vitamins and minerals. Let's look at hydration next. (No, not gin.)

Your blood runs through your veins, right? You want it to course freely, not dribble and stumble. The more hydrated you are, the more your blood will flow, possibly even gush, around your body delivering all those essentials goodies we've been talking about to the cells for nourishment. On the 21 Day Blast plan I am asking you to drink 2.5–3 litres of water per day. Every day. That means all the processes of your body will be running nicely. Not chugging or spluttering. More purring.

'What?! 3 litres?! Every day? I'll never get off the loo!'

Yes, you may wee like you never have before but you'll get a weird satisfaction from the glorious pale colour. Sort of newly mown hay, rather than sun-kissed straw. Add fresh lime or lemon chunks to your 3 litres to soften the blow; cucumber slices and mint also work well.

Make it a habit. Don't fight against it, just get on with it. You'll notice the difference in your skin, in your poo, your energy levels and in the puffiness of your fingers. If you don't drink enough, your body will hold on for grim death to what it's got and never let go. It will collect in unsightly pools around your ankles.

There's more about fluid and fluid retention in Chapter 5. I know . . . you can't wait.

Right, now let's find out how all these food facts can actually HELP us lose fat. On to Chapter 2.

Weight lost – 8lb
Inches lost – 9½ (bloody hell!)
Dress size reached – 12
Skin – glowing
Bladder – never seen so much action
Happiness – 10 out of 10
C.W., Bournemouth

Chapter 2

USING FOOD TO HELP US LOSE FAT

'My eating has improved so much. My plate is now full and I don't pick between meals. I used to think two rice cakes and some cottage cheese was a good lunch. I think I'd cry now if someone offered me that.'

A.N., Reading

HOW OUR BODIES GET FAT IN THE FIRST PLACE

In order to get into shape on the outside, it's what we do on the inside that counts. We've talked about food groups – here we're going to look at how those food groups; work together to give us great handfuls of fat where we don't want them – if we're not careful. And how we can manipulate our food to ensure they disappear.

The food we eat is broken down for easy transport in the bloodstream to the places that need it. Proteins are broken down into amino acids, carbohydrate into glucose and fats into fatty acids. Too much of any of these can make us fat.

'So it's not just the fat we eat that makes those handfuls of fat?'

No. Protein and carbohydrate play their part.

However, balance *can* be achieved. Read on.

Where we hold our fat depends very much on which sex hormones we have – that is, testosterone and oestrogen. By and large, men tend to hold fat in the abdominal area and women on their hips, thighs and back. All of it is made up of swollen fat cells. (Their posh name is triglycerides). When we talk about losing fat, we are essentially trying to release the fat from those bulging fat cells and set it free into the bloodstream. It then becomes known as free fatty acids and this is the fuel we should be using for all activity if we want a healthy body. So, emptying those fat cells means smaller handfuls of fat.

'Oooh, goody.'

But there's a hitch.

PERSUADING THE BODY TO GIVE UP THAT FAT

So if you remember, when you eat carbohydrate it gets converted to glucose and the hormone insulin carries it off to the cells that need it.

The body would much rather use that glucose for its energy than tap into your fat stores, mainly because it requires less effort to transport the glucose than it does to 'persuade' the fat from the fat cells.

The trouble comes if your diet is big on carbohydrate (the potatoes, oats, pasta, sugary goodies, cakes, chocolate . . . shall I go on?), then there will be an excess of glucose. Once insulin has finished delivering the glucose to the right places, it turns its attention to this excess. It sweeps it up, and stuffs it into the fat cells where it joins those triglycerides.

So, bigger fat cells again . . . and tighter trousers.

Not only that. Remember the free fatty acids . . . they're the usable form of our fat wodges floating around in the bloodstream begging to be used up. But oh no. When insulin scoops up the surplus glucose it also takes with it those free fatty acids and they're returned to the fat cells to become triglycerides again.

Our love handles.

So, broadly speaking, that's the story. Carbohydrate gets converted into glucose and is transported to the cells that need it. If we eat too much of it (think sofa, telly, large bag of sweets) and don't use it up, then insulin scoops up the excess, along with the free fatty acids and stuffs it all back into the fat cells. In places we don't want it.

Result: Your fat cells swell. Your jeans get tight. You feel lethargic and downright cross.

'So how can food help me release the fat from my fat cells . . . and use it up? Are you saying I should give up carbs?'

Definitely not. Imagine life without it. Your brain would be starved, you'd be drowsy and actually quite miserable. No, instead we're going to be eating the right kind and the right amount of carbohydrate, and at the right time.

Remember there are different sorts of carbohydrate. As we saw in Chapter 1, the ones that create a quick response from insulin are simple carbs – that's sugary foods, some fruit and processed foods. They are converted to glucose very quickly and prompt a surge of insulin. The other type are more complex (vegetables, whole-grains, brown rice, oats, potatoes), which take longer to be digested and won't trigger such a flood of insulin into your bloodstream.

Our plan is this: To stick to eating a lovely mix of protein and fats plus enough complex carbohydrate at the right time. When you exercise, your muscles need glucose and so afterwards your supplies are pretty low. Eating carbohydrate after exercise will ensure that those supplies are refilled. This will also help the muscles recover. And that's what we're going to do on Blast. Cue very important statement . . .

You will eat a portion of starchy carbs ONLY in the meal that follows your workout. The glucose produced from that meal will then be enough to top up your newly emptied stores. The rest of the time, the body will depend on those free fatty acids to fuel it through the rest of the day. This means a) no excess glucose being handcuffed to your fat cells and making them bigger, and b) the free fatty acids can roam freely in your bloodstream waiting to be used up.

Result: Smaller fat cells. Smaller trousers.

DIGGING A BIT DEEPER . . .

In our quest for external loveliness, we need to ensure internal harmony. Which means taking care of our gut. The gut basically goes from the bottom of the stomach to the anus and has two segments, the small intestine and the large intestine. This part of our bodies is not just responsible for breaking down our food into manageable particles and then expelling the waste (with some gurgling noises and nasty smells). No, the gut has been hailed as our 'second brain' and it seems that, through the billions of good healthy bacteria, the part it plays in the balance and stability of our emotions – and the impact it has on our personalities – is huge. It is not merely a place for digestion.

Essentially, a happy gut is central to our wellbeing.

If we are going to commit to eating food that will help us lose weight, then it is important our gut responds well to that food. If, every day we experience bloating, gas and gurgling plus a host of other unexplained symptoms (such as fungal issues, abdominal pain, lethargy) then our fat-loss progress will be hindered. This will also affect our mood and emotions. We are aiming for a digestive system that is calm and stable. And our mood will follow suit. If some foods create adverse reactions in the body, then we're looking at turbulent and rocky.

Before we get stuck into the 21 Day Blast plan rules, foods and workouts, let's just take a look at those foods that can jeopardise our gut harmony and therefore inhibit our fat loss.

I doubt any of them will be a surprise to you. They appear on our daily menus, dragging their stigmas and bad reputations behind them, and for good reason.

Chapter 3

THREATS TO GUT HARMONY

. . . and therefore to successful fat loss

Throughout the 21 Day Blast plan, the food you will be eating will help you lose fat, feel energised and be ready for anything. Your sweet cravings will diminish and your mood will stabilise. Your skin will glow, your sleep will be deep and your energy levels will rocket. However, there are some areas of food that do the opposite to all that. Take them away and – after an initial feeling of deprivation – you will then notice a whopping difference to your wellbeing and your mood.

I'm going to take you through those foods now. I promise you this isn't dull. I might even go as far as to say some of it is riveting.

SUGAR

Sugar is a simple form of carbohydrate and can be found in many foods: fruit juices, dressings, marinades, anything marked low-fat, fizzy drinks, sweets, biscuits, breakfast cereals, alcohol . . . the list goes on and on. It is broken down into glucose in the bloodstream. Too much of it, as we've seen, will be cemented in place as body fat.

Sugar is a drug and it needs a management programme. Cue the 21 Day Blast plan.

Research studies show that regular consumption of sugary products contributes to heart disease, rheumatoid arthritis and Alzheimer's; it increases the risk of diabetes, ruins our skin, makes us edgy and sends our hormones into overdrive. So in the wake of persistent bouts of biscuit-eating pleasure, there lies a serious and disastrous state of affairs.

Robert Lustig in his book *Fat Chance: The Hidden Truth About Sugar, Obesity and Disease* states that the damage done by 150-calories' worth of sugary fizzy drink far outweighs the damage done by 150 calories' worth of other food. Food for fat loss is not always about calories. It's about what those calories are made up of.

To help us understand more, look at it this way. Sugar comes in various forms, one of them is fructose. This is the sugar contained in fruit. When this is concentrated, it will raise glucose levels far beyond what we need.

More disturbing is that fructose is used in the making of sweeteners like agave syrup and maple syrup. These sweeteners, which you thought were natural, so unrefined, so back-to-nature, are added to food items to make them tempting, and seemingly healthy. Take some granolas for example. That very word smacks of crunchy, wholesome country kitchen, doesn't it?

There's a point to all this. Keep reading.

Around the 1970s the word on the street was that fat made you fat. This in turn led to a demand for products labelled low-fat. Following high tariffs on foreign sugar, a product called high fructose corn syrup (HFCS) was developed in the US. It was cheap, easy to make and it was used to replace the fat in many foods, ensuring food kept its taste and appeal to the public. The bonus was that it lengthened its shelf life.

Hence the birth of 'low-fat' products, and anything labelled as such became a fast seller: flavoured yoghurt, cereals, low-fat biscuits, cakes, sweets, breads, salad dressings, frozen convenience foods, fizzy drinks.

It was the addition of HFCS that made them edible and addictive. With their new low-fat status, these foods flew off the shelves; the public were jubilant and couldn't get enough. The more they ate, the more they wanted to eat. And so the gentle (and now stratospheric) rise in human obesity levels began.

This means that it is easy for our taste buds to become wired to enjoy sweetness. We become used to it. We long for it. We can't stop thinking about it. Eventually we give in.

'Oh, you're all good news and merry cheer, aren't you? Does that mean I can never have anything sugary or processed ever again? Ever?'

God no. It just means finding balance. Occasional 'Oh sod it' moments are inevitable in life. Moments when you crack open a bottle of Merlot, chuck a supermarket pizza in the oven and throw caution to the wind . . . they're wonderful! On Blast we are going to learn how not to allow sugar to run our lives and govern our food choices. We are going to train our taste buds to love real food, cook real food (no gourmet chef-ness required) and leave our sweet tooth dribbling by the wayside. So in the long run, that pizza may not become so regular . . . or so enticing.

ON BLAST: The only sugar you will have is sugar that naturally appears in carbohydrate-rich foods such as oats, potatoes and some fruits. As an example there is 0.8g of sugar in 100g of potato. And there is 6.4g sugar in a Jaffa cake biscuit. (One whole teaspoon of sugar is 5g.)

Just thought I'd put that out there.

On to something else . . .

'Day 4: I know it's early days but I am starting to feel so much better. I keep going to tap my tummy and it's shrinking! Can't say I haven't thought about a bar of chocolate but I'm not craving it like my life depended on it and I feel at ease with my life, calm and present. Very weird, but good weird.'

B.S., London

WHEAT

Wheat has long been known as an irritant to the digestive system and it has become very fashionable to give it up. Masses of research has been done and very little of it conclusive. But it does appear that avoiding wheat products can make us feel better. Is this because so many wheat-based products are manufactured with additives and chemicals in order to prolong their shelf life? This would mean the body finds it difficult to process these chemicals, putting a strain on the liver. This results in toxins being stored in fat cells. Or is it due to the gluten present in wheat?

Gluten is a protein present not only in wheat but also in rye, barley and in a small amount in oats. If you have a full-blown allergy to gluten (and here I mean constant stomach pains, diarrhoea, gas, vomiting) then you may be a sufferer of coeliac disease. This is when the gut and the intestinal wall become damaged and inflamed. It is a serious condition and if you think it applies to you, then get yourself to a doctor pretty pronto, as it must be treated by medical professionals.

One can have an allergy or sensitivity to wheat without being gluten intolerant. The results can be difficult to diagnose due to delayed reaction times and the range and severity of symptoms, but these can be anything from sneezing, wheezing, itching and rashes to digestive issues, sore joints and limbs and nausea. More chronic conditions are migraines, irritable bowel syndrome and arthritis. All of these are often alleviated by the replacement of wheat with other forms of carbohydrate.

Milder forms of wheat intolerance can manifest themselves with bloating, headaches and hay fever-like symptoms. Wheat-based products such as spongy bread and pasta can absorb a lot of water and swell in the body, causing a bloated feeling, which is why many feel so much better (and flatter!) on a wheat-free regime. Yeast can also be a culprit, so if you are a big bread eater, it may be this that is causing your discomfort, too.

You may not know whether you have an intolerance or a full-blown allergy or neither until you omit wheat from your daily diet, but you are likely to feel different over the course of the 21 days without it. A high proportion of the bread and cakes we eat these days is quite highly processed and so opting for more natural forms of carbs (rice, potatoes, sweet potatoes, quinoa) will put less strain on the gut and we will ultimately feel better for that.

It's worth mentioning that supermarkets today have developed whole sections devoted to gluten-free products and you might be tempted to skip down those aisles and fill up your trolley. Be very wary of these. They tend to be expensive, full of unpronounceable ingredients and loaded with sugar. The label gluten-free does not necessarily mean it is good for you. It just means what it says . . . free of gluten.

ON BLAST: For 21 days you are going to go without wheat-based products. So, that's biscuits, bread, crackers, cakes and pasta. This includes all bread-related items, which you may deem as totally scrumptious, like tortilla wraps, pittas and focaccia. Anything spongy and squidgy, which may make your gut . . . erm . . . spongy and squidgy. If you are a lover of pasta, then there are many non-wheat varieties on the market – these are mentioned in the Blast rules in Part 2 of the book.

DAIRY

There is untold research available about the effects of cow's milk products on the human digestive system, and as with wheat products, some of it is inconclusive. You may regard all of this as poppycock, and you may be tempted to put down your IBS, aching joints, migraines, arthritis, sinus and mucus issues, flatulence and skin disorders to other factors. (I'm continuing with the merry cheer . . . have you noticed?)

Fat, as we have seen, is broken down into fatty acids for easy transport in the blood. You can tell different fatty acids apart in many different ways without getting into long, dull explanations. One of those is looking at the length of the 'chains' within those fatty acids. Take cow's and goat's milk. The fat in cow's milk contains long-chain fatty acids, which us humans can find difficult to digest. Goat's milk has shorter chains and therefore some find this easier on the system.

None of it can be proved, but it's worth trying alternatives. I remember my daughter had terrible eczema as a three year old, and switching to goat's milk for a year completely got rid of it. Good alternatives to animal dairy are (don't wince) unsweetened almond milk, rice milk, soya milk, coconut milk and hemp milk. These are worth trying for very little expense and your gut may welcome the change. In the recipe section of the book, these milks are sometimes referred to as non-dairy or dairy-free.

One exception to our Blast cow's dairy rule is good Greek yoghurt. This is because live cultures are added to the cow's milk in the yoghurt-making process, which not only renders the product miles more digestible but actually benefits the bacteria* that live in our gut and which we need to nurture.

Why Greek? For no particular reason other than that the high-protein, low-sugar (less than 4g per 100g) varieties are usually labelled as Greek yoghurt. The brand TOTAL would be hailed as queen of the bunch, but it is often quite expensive and there are some other very good, cheaper brands available such as SKYR. Search around but have your 'label detective' wits about you. They often contain very poor levels of protein and whopping amounts of sugar.

It's worth singling out one of the non-dairy options here: soya milk. Soy-based products (soya milk, tofu, etc.) are a great source of protein as they contain the whole package of 20 amino acids as well as valuable omega-3 fats, B vitamins and iron. They also contain phytoestrogens, which act in the same way as the female hormone oestrogen but to a much milder degree. For this reason, much has been written about their ability to alleviate symptoms of the menopause, prevent some cancers and boost libido. It is therefore tempting to knock back the soya milk and anything else containing these phyto things (they are present in a range of foods – tempeh, flaxseeds, oats, barley, lentils, liquorice root, sweet potato).

* This friendly bacteria is known as microflora and we've all got it. It lives in our mouths and noses but mostly in our gut, and en masse these friendly bacteria weigh about 1.5kg. It is vital in helping us absorb antioxidants from food, building our defences and maintaining our immune system for life. The gut is home to both friendly and hostile bacteria and the optimum is said to be around an 85:15 balance. Factors such as diet, environment, infections, antibiotics, stress, lack of sleep and ageing can all upset this balance.

All of this may indeed be valid, but I wouldn't be doing my job properly as a health and fitness professional if I didn't say this. Some cancers (such as breast cancer) have been linked to high levels of oestrogen and therefore medical experts recommend that post-menopausal women with a link to oestrogen-dependent breast cancer should be vigilant about their consumption of soya products and other products that contain phytoestrogens and take good medical advice.

My personal advice would be to do your own research. There is much evidence/research (inconsequential and otherwise) about the risks of over-consumption of soya, not only for the menopausal sector but also for those who are trying for babies or who are pregnant.

If all that has made you fearful, then opt for one of the other choices. I personally dance between coconut milk, unsweetened almond milk and goat's, with the odd splash of soya.

ON BLAST: For 21 days you are recommended to use other non-dairy milks instead of cow's milk. You can do as much lip-curling and face-pulling as you like, but give it a go. You'll be surprised.

CAFFEINE

'Oh, not the coffee . . . no! Not the cappuccino . . . Please don't take that away . . .'

Years back, I remember meeting a woman at the beginning of her Blast journey, who confessed to drinking fifteen cups of tea a day. Minimum. And possibly more if her day was going pear-shaped. By the end of the 21 days she had completely lost the 21-fags-a-day look, the dark circles had disappeared and her skin was smooth, almost glowing. She had lost ten years. I was stunned by the difference and oh how I wish I'd taken a photo.

One good fresh coffee (or other highly caffeinated drink) per day does this: it kick-starts the system by temporarily raising your heart rate and blood pressure. It also stimulates the release of the hormone dopamine, which reduces fatigue. In short, you'll feel upbeat, bouncy, possibly even perky. And that will be enough perk to get you through the day.

The flipside of the caffeine coin is when you consistently drink too much of it. Your blood pressure is permanently increased, your heart is thumping and the body senses a stressful situation. A message is then sent to the adrenal glands to produce the hormone cortisol. Cortisol then helps the body deal with the stress by providing the muscles with large amounts of glucose (it does this by tapping into protein stores via a process called gluconeogenesis in the liver). This glucose is supposed to help the body deal with the 'fight or flight' mode (i.e. run like hell or stick it out and do battle). But of course, this is only the physiological response and there is no need for fight or flight.

The upshot of the pretend stress caused by the quaffing of caffeine is a continuous wave of glucose. Which isn't being used up and which is packed off to the fat cells by insulin.

Not only that . . .

'Oh for heaven's sake, isn't that enough?'

. . . we are striving for an even keel in the hormone department and now the blood is flooded with cortisol and insulin. If the body has to produce more than usual amounts of one hormone, then that upsets the activities of the others. More about the dismal effects of hormone imbalances can be read in Chapter 4.

ON BLAST: You are permitted one caffeinated drink a day during the course of the plan. This will set you up and get you going. We want calm. We want happy. Not raging and furious.

ALCOHOL

Our modern-day culture means most of us enjoy a drink to unwind, to socialise and to let rip. It tastes good, our guard drops, our rough edges are softened and we feel nice. Fluffy and at peace with the world. That's on the outside. On the inside, it's a different story.

There's no getting away from it . . . alcohol is a toxin. And a toxin is 'related to or caused by poison', according to the *Oxford English Dictionary*. So when you've necked back your first few mojitos, the body sends in the troops. Cortisol is produced to sweep the alcohol from the blood and pack it off to the liver to be metabolised. It's urgent. It takes priority. It's a toxin after all.

'Sounds like good news, no?'

No. The converted alcohol can now be used as fuel for energy, instead of that glucose or those fatty acids wandering about your bloodstream. The body puts the brakes on using up fat and glucose and any other fuel EXCEPT the alcohol.

Oh . . . wait. There's more. All that sugar in the alcohol means insulin is also being produced, which can only mean one thing. The insulin packs off that sugar and the fatty acids back into the fat cells until the alcohol has been used up.

So, you may be feeling totally relaxed, groovy and chilled, but your liver is under pressure, you've just made some more fat, and the fat you had in the first place isn't being used up either.

It's not looking good, is it? On top of that, you've got a massive headache looming.

So, cutting down on alcohol is a hard nut to crack but the effects will show in your health, your blood pressure and your waistline, not to mention your skin.

ON BLAST: So, we're not going to imbibe on the 21 Day Blast plan. No, we're going to be alcohol-free for the entire 21 days so that you can give your body a rest. Your head and conscience will also get some downtime since the 'shall I, shan't I?' conflict won't be mixed up with the 'I shouldn't, should I? . . . it's only Tuesday' dilemma. There's one answer. No, you won't.

Remember, we are looking for calm and happy with a disciplined mind. Not toxin-dependent with no willpower and your head in a family bag of Doritos. Dull and boring? Possibly . . . at first. Effective and long-lasting? Definitely. The lethal combination of sugar and alcohol results in calamity for one's self-discipline. Prosecco and beer will never taste as good as smug and saintly feel.

During the Blast plan I am giving your body (and your head) the chance to break some old habits over 21 days. Once the 21 days are over, you'll have discovered the benefits of change and then you can decide a plan of action to take you forward. You'll find more about our post-Blast plan later in the book.

For now, let's head to the next chapter and have a look at hormones. They're not all bad news. Far from it.

Chapter 4

THE PART HORMONES PLAY IN FAT LOSS

I'm not talking those little friends who raise their heads once a month (maybe more!) and who have the potential to turn us women from sane and normal people operating with dignity and maturity into bonkers and irrational types who fail to master even the smallest of tasks.

To be successful in fat loss we have to understand what we're up against. You can be in control of your food through the 21 Day Blast plan guidelines (see Chapter 5) but we are less in control of our hormones.

WHAT ARE HORMONES?

Broadly speaking, hormones are chemical substances, secreted by our glands, which are transported in the blood to different organs. These hormones, along with the messages they carry, control most major bodily functions. Hormones work together, so an over-plentiful supply of one may mean that another is out of balance, too. There are about fifty different hormones (some I can't even pronounce) and it is impossible to find out whether they are all doing their jobs correctly, and to the full advantage of our health, our fat stores and our energy levels.

BUT – and this is where I get on my soapbox – everything you will be doing on the 21 Day Blast plan will go a long way to helping keep the main players working with, rather than fighting against, each other and therefore maintaining the efficiency of the fat-loss process. Let's look at the main characters.

INSULIN

We learnt about insulin in Chapter 2. By way of a quick recap, it's produced in the pancreas in response to eating carbohydrate, which is converted to glucose and which insulin delivers to the cells that need it. Any excess glucose remaining unused is swept up by the insulin and stuffed into our fat cells. Essentially, the more glucose, the more insulin, the bigger our fat cells.

How can we ensure insulin stays at the optimum level?

By eating carbohydrates only after exercise – this is the point when the body most needs them. Simply speaking, this will mean that just enough insulin is produced to send just enough glucose to the brain and to those muscles (which you've just worked). The lack of spare insulin and spare glucose means that the body unlocks the fat from our fat cells (previously held under lock and key by all that insulin) and turns it into free fatty acids for use as fuel.

Empty fat cells, here we come.

CORTISOL

This hormone is produced in the adrenal glands and affects many different tasks around the body, simply because most cells in the body are equipped with cortisol receptors. This means it can affect the harmony of other hormones too, so when cortisol production is steady and drama-free, there's a good chance other hormone levels will also fall into line.

Cortisol is produced in response to stress and this is vital. It provides the body with glucose in order to be able to deal with trauma, illness, fright, infection, bleeding and high blood pressure, among others. Cortisol gets hold of this glucose very quickly (remember, there's a panic on!) by breaking down protein stores in the liver.

However, our modern-day culture means that we are subject to constant stressful situations, both emotional and physical: work deadlines, traffic, noise, disharmony in relationships, diets that don't satisfy our body's needs and too little exercise. This can mean a build-up of cortisol as it strives to produce enough glucose in order to cope with this stress.

High levels of cortisol mean more glucose. Too much glucose means more insulin, which means our fat storing is easier and burning that fat is harder. It's locked back up in those fat cells!

Being stressed at the same time as eating a high-sugar, high-carb diet is the worst combination for your health, your fat-loss plans and your hormone harmony. Big stress equals big trousers.

How can we ensure cortisol stays at an optimum level?

Wakeful nights put the body under huge stress so try and regulate your cortisol production by getting enough sleep. Take the pressure off your body by feeding it foods that won't cause a fight. Take regular exercise, possibly with a friend whose company nourishes your very soul. Go easy on the caffeine and alcohol, but large on sleep and vegetables.

All that sounds like the life of someone truly dull, doesn't it? Shall we rewrite that? Enjoy some lazy lie-ins, swap your coffee for chamomile tea, laugh out loud at every opportunity and do a little dance . . . like you just don't care. You'll be doing all that on Blast. Yes, including the little dance. Daily!

TESTOSTERONE

An image of bulging muscles has just entered your head, hasn't it? Fake tan, oily chest, ripped abs, the works.

All of us need a dose of this little hormone. It's not only produced in the male testes but also in the adrenal glands and ovaries of the female. As we approach the menopause (up to as much as ten years before) it's not only oestrogen levels that drop off but testosterone too.

Testosterone helps keeps our muscles firm and taut. It also stimulates our urge for the occasional swing from the chandelier, should the fancy take us. So, come the menopause, we risk not only droopy muscles but a droopy libido.

It's not looking good.

So how can we keep testosterone at an optimum level?

Use those muscles! That means challenging them and taking them ever so slightly out of their comfort zone. Muscles mean strength. Toned muscles mean well-supported joints and a strong framework. Toned muscles require energy to keep them in that toned state, so we are burning fat even while we're sitting still.

So, using your muscles keeps testosterone levels up. That means your libido and energy levels are up too, but your fat levels are kept down. I'm making it sound very simple, aren't I? Do some squats, eat some broccoli, bring on the Friday-night love-in.

(I'm going to say something slightly toe-curling: testosterone is also responsible for the sensitivity of the nipples and clitoris. There. Finished.)

So, the Blast plan will help us keep the levels of these three important hormones stable.

Remember, too, that they work together, so if insulin, cortisol and testosterone are affected positively, then it's very likely that they will have a knock-on effect in other areas.

GHRELIN & LEPTIN

This double act is definitely worth a mention. They are the big players in terms of regulating appetite . . . which then has a knock-on effect on our body shape

Ghrelin is a hormone produced mainly in the stomach. It's known as the 'hunger hormone' because it stimulates appetite, increases food intake and promotes fat storage. It actually tells us to eat (as if we need telling). For successful fat loss we need ghrelin levels to be low so that we aren't tempted by hunger pangs.

On very low-calorie diets, ghrelin levels rise and stay raised. Once the diet is abandoned (as they usually are because you find yourself chewing the furniture), wham . . . ghrelin sets to work on your appetite, the pounds pile back on and you're left with higher fat levels than you started with.

Leptin does the opposite. Leptin is a hormone produced in the fat cells and it controls metabolism, hunger and energy expenditure. It tells us to stop eating. The larger you are (in terms of fat-ness) the more leptin you will produce.

'Brilliant. I won't be fat for long because I will soon magically stop eating because of all that leptin.'

However, the danger comes when the brain eventually becomes numb to leptin's messages. There is no longer anything to tell you to stop

eating. This is called leptin resistance. There is no drop in appetite and no 'I'm full' signals, so you just keep eating.

So how can we ensure leptin and ghrelin stay at an optimum level? For successful fat loss, we need leptin levels to be high and ghrelin levels to be low. Stay away from low-calorie diets because they are unsustainable. They make us miserable and put the body under stress (cue cortisol) and are a disaster both for health and fat loss. We must focus on eating foods our body was designed to use and not processed goods that have been altered chemically, which our bodies won't recognise. These foods create a toxic environment in the blood, and, as our years advance, do their hardest to prevent us from living the life we want to lead.

Get me, coming over all serious . . .

We all have our own unique hormone profile but no single hormone can control our fat levels or our appetite. Fuelling your body with the Blast food guidelines will give you the chance to help those hormones work *with* you.

Committing to a nutrient-rich and balanced diet of protein, fat and carbohydrate at the right time and avoiding those foods that risk causing a rumpus, a scuffle or a full-on brawl in your gut will keep everything swinging along nicely. Enough glucose is produced to feed the cells, the hormones are doing their hormone-thing calmly and no one is hungry.

There. I've finished waving the hormone stick for the moment, but I'm sure it'll make an appearance later on. Let's crack on with the next chapter and find out exactly what those Blast guidelines are.

THE BLAST EATING PLAN & RECIPES

2

THE FOOD, THE RULES, THE TOOLS

Chapter 5

THE BLAST PLAN FOOD GUIDELINES (or ... what to eat and when)

'Day 6: I've not had a single mid-afternoon slump since starting. Usually 3pm rolls around and I'm using cocktail sticks to keep my eyes open. I've been a bouncing ball of energy and it's fantastic!'

C.W., London

Two words: nourish and flourish. This is the juicy bit, the bit where you learn the simple Blast eating guidelines and where you will be inspired by the gorgeous recipes and meal ideas, all perfectly suited to everyday family life.

The results of eating the Blast way for 21 days will surprise you. Together with the effects from the workouts, you will soon start to feel different, energetic and, dare I say it, really quite wonderful.

The Blast plan makes losing fat easier because the food you eat will encourage your body to use up its fat stores. Carbohydrate consumption is offset by four short workouts per week, which gives us minimum glucose, stable insulin levels plus a newfound fitness and rock-hard thighs.

You're going to take your body on a holiday, where it can relax and breathe, away from hassle and turmoil. You're going to get control back.

Let's look at the instructions. They're clear and straightforward. We haven't got time for complicated.

HOW & WHAT CAN I EAT?

In Chapters 3 and 4 we learnt how some foods can aggravate the gut and risk causing hormonal upheaval. We're going to take a rest from these. See Section A, overleaf.

Sections B and C tell you about the foods that are permitted in the plan, together with the guidelines surrounding those foods. There are also sample meal day-planners.

I've also included a summary (which is code for me making absolutely sure that YOU are absolutely sure).

Section D gives guidance on portion size.

Section E is devoted to fluids.

See . . . no jokes. I've gone all sensible and grown-up.

A. FOODS NOT PERMITTED ON BLAST

- Wheat or any products containing wheat: Bread, cakes, biscuits, pastries, wheat-based pasta, etc.

- Cow's dairy: Milk, cream, butter, cheese. There is one exception. Unsweetened yoghurt contains live cultures, which are good for promoting healthy gut bacteria. Make sure the sugar content is low (less than 4g per 100g of product) and the protein content is as high as you can find (7g per 100g or higher). Greek yoghurt tends to hit the spot

- Sugar: Any products containing added sugar – which means cakes, fizzy drinks, biscuits, fruit juices, chocolate, cereals

Fruit is permitted but there are limits (see pages 56–7)

- Caffeine: One caffeinated drink per day is allowed

- Alcohol: It stops us losing fat, lowers our willpower and turns us into people who want to eat crisps

- All processed food: This means most ready meals, foods with a long shelf life, takeaways, convenience foods. (This doesn't mean your life is suddenly going to become inconvenient!)

B. THE BLAST GUIDELINES

1. You will eat normal, delicious food every day. Hold that thought.

2. Each day you will eat three meals plus one snack if you find you need it. These meals will be made up of *Anytime* foods and *After Workout* foods. Details of these are on pages 56–7.

3. Protein and fat: A good part of your meals will be made up of protein and fat. Getting a decent amount of protein in each meal is very important as this is going to preserve your newly found muscles; it will help keep you full and will minimise insulin response (see page 47). Fats are important for taste,

satiety and for the goodness they bring to the body (see Chapter 1).

4. Carbohydrate: You will also be eating a portion of starchy carbohydrate but *only* in the meal that follows a workout. Post-exercise, the body utilises the glucose much quicker and more efficiently, and there is less risk of a build-up of insulin. So, for example, if you do your workout mid-morning, then your lunch must include a portion of carbohydrate. If you plan on doing your workout in the evening after you've been to work, then you must have your carb portion with dinner.

- Vegetables: These are also classed as carbohydrate and you are allowed to pile your plate high with these (apart from the starchy ones. See the Food Lists on pages 56–7). This is for two reasons: one, to ensure a whopping dose of vitamins and minerals; two, to visually fill any gaps that, pre-Blast, may have been occupied by potatoes or pasta. No one wants gaps on plates.

C. WHEN TO EAT PERMITTED FOODS

On pages 56–7 you'll find the Food Lists. These will help you make up your meals. Section D, which gives you guidance on portion size, is there to ensure you have success, while the Recipes section, Chapter 8, will offer inspiration. They are there to help you create your own meal ideas but they are not compulsory. You can make your meals up from what you like, as long as you follow the Blast rules.

Anytime foods: During a large part of the 21 Day Blast plan, you will eat from the Anytime list. These are foods which don't feature starchy carbohydrates and you will make up all your meals from these ingredients (and from the Anytime recipe sections in Chapter 8), except the meal that follows a workout.

After Workout foods: This is a list of foods containing starchy carbohydrates. When you have done one of the Blast workouts (there are four to do each week), then you must add something from this list to the meal that follows that workout. Again, you can refer to the Recipes section and let your imagination run amok, or you can create and assemble simpler meals.

‘I'm 10 inches (and 9lb) down and feeling fabulous. I love Blast, it really works for me and I love the sensible-ness of it. Proper food, decent exercise and a healthy attitude to fitness, health and our bodies. Thank you, I'm spreading the word.’

H.W., London

THE ANYTIME FOOD LIST

These are the foods that you eat at the meals before a workout and on those days when you are not exercising at all. Please see pages 60–6 for portion-size information.

ALL FRESH UNPROCESSED MEAT	Beef, lamb, pork, chicken, turkey, duck, etc.
ALL FISH	Including shellfish (nothing with breadcrumbs or a non-natural coating pretending to be something exotic)
EGGS	For baking and cooking. Vegans may like to make a chia seed egg (see page 204)
GOOD RUSK- OR GLUTEN-FREE SAUSAGES	These should contain minimal sugar and a high meat content (more than 95%). There may be a small percentage of other padding such as rice flour or other starch, which is fine
CHORIZO	Again, look for a high meat content, low sugar, and keep portions small
BACON	As lean as possible. Just natural, not covered in a flavouring
PULSES AND BEANS	Chickpeas, lentils, split peas, all types of beans (kidney beans, cannellini beans, black beans, butter beans etc., tinned or dried)
TOFU	Including tempeh (fermented soya beans like tofu, but denser and more chewy) and plain Quorn products
YOGHURT	Natural unsweetened yoghurt, the higher protein the better
VEGETABLES	Apart from potatoes, sweet potatoes, butternut squash and parsnips (which are on the After Workout list), all vegetables and salad ingredients are permitted – the more the better! Peas, sweetcorn, beetroot, celeriac, cabbage, kale, broccoli, cucumber, rocket, carrots, peppers, cucumber, mushrooms . . . the list goes on and on
NUTS AND SEEDS – WITH CAUTION!	These make good snacks, but watch portion size. Obviously not the sticky caramel honey-roasted kind – just plain or roasted and salted
NUT BUTTERS	Almond or peanut (without palm oil or sugar). Take care – it's very easy to go to bed with the jar and a spoon
FRUIT	Tomatoes, avocados, plus low-carbohydrate fruits – which amounts to berries (raspberries, blackcurrants, blueberries, blackberries, strawberries), melons and peaches. A sprinkling of pomegranate seeds has been used on some of the Anytime salads, which is permissible. Other fruits are discussed on page 61, and dried fruit is not permitted at all
PROTEIN POWDER	A scoop (about 25g) of a non-dairy protein powder can really add power to your smoothies and your oats. Soy protein powder or a vegan mix containing other plant proteins are the best options. Avoid the whey protein powders, which have been artificially sweetened and flavoured – they're sickly and do weird things to your stomach. There's more about these on pages 83–5, in the store-cupboard section
OILS	Olive oil, sesame oil, walnut oil, avocado oil, coconut oil and rapeseed oil. Be sparing

HOT DRINKS	Coffee or tea (one per day) and then as many herbal teas and fruit teas as you can neck down
WATER	Lemons, limes, cucumber and mint are great for livening up still or fizzy water. Avoid shop-bought flavoured waters
ALTERNATIVES TO COW'S MILK	Unsweetened almond milk, soya milk, coconut milk, hemp milk. Goat's milk is also permitted although some find this a bit farmyard-y. It's much kinder to the digestive system than cow's
SAUCES AND SPICES	Soy sauces, tamari sauce, apple cider vinegar, sugar-free stock powder or cubes. Apple cider vinegar is very good in baking as it helps create fluffy muffins (see page 210). All herbs and spices can be used with gay abandon

THE AFTER WORKOUT FOOD LIST

This list contains carbohydrate-rich foods that must be eaten in the meal that directly follows one of your workouts. You choose one portion of these to add to anything in the Anytime list. Your body needs carbohydrate after exercise and that's exactly when you can have it.

OATS	And any other non-wheat grains such as amaranth, sorghum and teff, which, despite sounding like posh children's names, are actually non-wheat related grains with impressive nutritional stats. They can be cooked like quinoa or rice
QUINOA, RICE	All types and colours
BUCKWHEAT	The flour and groats have been used in some of the recipes. Coconut flour is also permitted
STARCHY VEGETABLES	Potatoes, sweet potatoes, butternut squash and parsnips
WHEAT-FREE PASTA	There are several varieties on the market, some more tasty than others. Be mindful of any sugar content
FRUIT	You are permitted one piece of 'after-workout' fruit (such as banana, pear, etc.) per day at any point during a workout day, either as a dessert or snack. This is in addition to the portion of low-carb fruit featured on the Anytime list of foods, and to your meal with carbohydrates that immediately follows a workout
BREAD MADE WITHOUT WHEAT	Rye bread and other good wheat-free varieties are permitted. Make your own if you can. See the recipe on page 108 for Courgette Bread – it's a dream

Remember, we are offsetting carbohydrate against exercise, to keep insulin levels low and produce just the right amount of glucose, which will encourage the body to use our fat stores for the rest of its fuel.

So, for example, say you did your Blast workout at around 11am. That means your next meal is lunch, which should contain carbohydrate (it will be an After Workout meal). Maybe a lovely chicken salad (lots of chicken, greens, tomatoes, basil, chuck on a few walnuts, a smidgen of olive oil), then add to that a jacket potato, some rice salad or a slice of rye bread, whatever you like.

Just to be sure the rules are clear and cemented in your mind, here are examples of a day's eating for both a Non-Workout Day and a Workout Day. Remember, it is up to you when you do your workout – whatever suits your schedule – but your carb portion must be included in the meal that follows that workout.

The suggestions given are exactly that, only suggestions. You make up your meal the way you like, according to the Blast guidelines and using the meal ideas and recipes in the Recipes section (Chapter 8).

THE NON-WORKOUT DAY

You will eat Anytime foods.

THE WORKOUT DAY

You will eat Anytime foods apart from the meal that follows your workout. That will be an After Workout meal (or an Anytime meal with a portion of carbs added).

Have a look at the table opposite. Remember, these are only suggestions. They are not prescriptive.

THE SUMMARY

- You eat three meals every day. Add a snack to that if you find you are still hungry.

- You do four Blast workouts per week. They're only short!

- You drink 3 litres of fluid per day (your teas and coffee count too, but this is a great opportunity to get into a good water routine).

- You eat from the Anytime list (or use the Anytime recipes), except for the meal that follows a workout, when you eat from the After Workout list (or use the After Workout recipes).

	EXAMPLE OF A NON-WORKOUT DAY	EXAMPLE OF A WORKOUT DAY (Assuming you have done a workout before breakfast)
BREAKFAST	2 rusk-free sausages, a grilled tomato and mushrooms sautéed in olive oil and thyme Or Greek yoghurt, 10–15 almonds, a handful of raspberries and blueberries (and a sprinkle of cinnamon . . . lovely!)	(With carbs) Banana and Peanut Overnight Oats (see page 113) Or If savoury suits you better, then try scrambled eggs on a piece of rye toast
LUNCH	(In the office) Large box filled with a large chopped chicken breast, a dollop of homemade guacamole, some chunky oven-roasted vegetables all on a bed of rocket and spinach, plus some berries or a few nuts for pud (At home) Turkey (or beef) burgers with some homemade coleslaw (see page 126), salad and one of the lovely dips in Sides, Dips & Relishes, pages 183–97	(In the office) A lunchbox containing two gluten-free sausages, a chicken drumstick and a pile of chickpea stew (just hog the office microwave) with some leftover veg from last night Blueberries and 10–15 cashew nuts for pud (At home) A two-egg omelette filled with a small slice of smoked salmon and dill with tomatoes, cucumber and piles of rocket A banana (that's your Workout Day fruit) plus some Greek yoghurt
SNACK (only if needed, not because you're bored)	Curried Bean Patties (see page 204) with a cucumber dip or a bowl of an Anytime soup	A Mini Sweet Potato and Bacon Frittata (see page 110) and some cherry tomatoes
DINNER	Lamb steaks, carrots, broccoli and peas, plain or jazzed up with a drizzle of oil and some rosemary All washed down with a hot decaf tea and a snooze on the sofa	Smoked paprika chicken with piles of green vegetables and carrots A cup of your favourite tea (you will have discovered lots of decaf varieties)
FLUID	2.5–3 litres water/hot drinks	2.5–3 litres water/hot drinks

D. PORTION SIZES

You are now armed with information about what to eat, so here we tackle the matter of how much. Portion control is often the blot on the fat-loss landscape, so we need to exercise some caution.

Weighing foods sounds tiresome, but you'll only need to do it a couple of times at first then it'll be tattooed on your brain for ever more. A range of weights has been given for some of the foods – make a sensible choice according to your height and size.

ANYTIME FOODS

Meat/fish/seafood: Around 150–200g portion, roughly the size of your fist

Bacon: Two rashers at any meal (maximum three times per week, due to the high salt content)

Chorizo: No, not great hunks torn off caveman-style. About 25g diced to add to omelettes, stews and salads

Eggs: Two or three at a time. To bulk them out, you can add liquid egg white, available from supermarkets in a carton

Fruit: Blueberries, blackcurrants, raspberries, blackberries, strawberries and other low-carb fruit such as peaches and melon – 100g at any one time (or two lots of 50g)

Chickpeas, lentils, kidney beans, cannellini beans and all other beans: 75–100g, cooked, per portion

Permitted vegetables: With green vegetables (spinach, broccoli, cabbage, spring greens, courgettes, asparagus) go ahead and fill your boots. Be more cautious with the starchy ones like sweetcorn and peas. Around 3 tablespoons is about right

Nuts: They are very filling but very calorie-dense so the guidelines are 10–15 almonds or cashew nuts or 6–10 Brazil nuts or walnut halves. For other nuts, use the size of these as a rough guide. Pathetically precise, I know, but nuts feel like a luxury, a treat, and great handfuls will not a Blast goddess make

Seeds: Tempting to sprinkle from the packet but use a teaspoon instead. One teaspoon of sunflower, pumpkin or sesame seeds scattered on salads, yoghurt or porridge adds a dose of good fat and a little nutty crunch

Greek yoghurt: 100–200g at any one time if this makes up the bulk of your, say, breakfast. Have up to 100g if you are using this as a second course or snack. You can spoon a dessertspoonful mixed with mustard and herbs on to salads or meat courses to make a good dip or dressing and it also pads out guacamole and hummus. Ensure as far as possible that the sugar content is below 4g per 100g of product and that the protein quota is as high as you can find – about 7g per 100g is good

Milk: Almond milk, rice milk, soya milk, coconut milk, all unsweetened, or other unsweetened plant or nut milks. Use whatever you need, mixed with water, for porridge and smoothies. Add a splash of your favourite to your hot drinks

Fats for cooking: Get into teaspoon mode! Coconut oil (the hard white stuff in a jar), rapeseed oil and olive oil are best for cooking and 1 teaspoon (5g) is often enough for a meal for two. Half a teaspoon of coconut oil is ample.

For drizzling use olive oil (tastes the nicest) and you can mix it with vinegar or lemon juice and a little mustard for a salad dressing – 1 teaspoon of oil is ample here

Caffeinated drinks: One per day

Decaffeinated coffees and teas: Brands that use a water-only decaffeinating process are best and you may drink these without any limits. Those using chemical solvents to take the caffeine out should be limited to two or three per day

Herbal teas and water: Lots! See section E below on fluids

AFTER WORKOUT FOODS

Oats or oats mixed with other non-wheat grains: 60–80g dry weight

Rye bread/buckwheat bread: Two slices

Rice, quinoa, other grains: 100–120g cooked weight. Ensure you wash quinoa grains before cooking. I've used buckwheat flour in some of the recipes – just follow the quantities given

Sweet potatoes/potatoes/parsnip/ butternut squash: One portion, around 200g in weight

Other fruit: One per day, on exercise days, so one large banana, one large apple, one large slice of pineapple. Large . . . that's a good word

E. FLUIDS

Serious hat on: it's very important that you take in enough to avoid fluid retention.

'Oh wait for it . . . she's going to bang on about water . . . horrible, boring, cold water.'

Yes, I'm afraid I am. But let's not look upon it as boring – more an oiling of the fat-losing machinery.

Our blood is 90 per cent water, our muscles are about 70 per cent water and even our bones contain 20 per cent. Every physiological process in your body needs water: digestion, circulation, respiration, absorption, metabolising of fat (yes, even that), joint lubrication and excretion.

Toxic waste products (and we're hoping to get rid of a few of those) are eliminated from the body with the help of the kidneys via urine. They will need good supplies of fluids to do that. We are going to be nourishing our bodies with great food and working hard to make it efficient at fat burning. Why jeopardise all that by not giving your body what it needs?

So we need to try and get 2.5–3 litres of fluid down our necks each day.

You might struggle at first, but like everything here, it's just a habit that your body will adapt to. You can supplement the 'cold boring water' with herbal teas. Never in a million years did I think I would be supping something which has 'A radiant blend of organic nettle, fennel and

peppermint' on the packet, but it's actually very hydrating and scores big points on the smug-o-meter.

So fill up your bottle, keep it handy and glug away

. . . and keep an eye out for the nearest toilet.

You will feel clean and pure. Holy even . . . OK, maybe that's pushing it.

MAKING A START

So, you've read what the Blast plan requires you to do in terms of changes to your food . . .

'Yes I have. I need a lie-down . . .'

The foods you are going to be eating will nourish you. There will be fewer irritants to the gut (sugar, animal dairy, alcohol, wheat, caffeine) and enough carbohydrate to keep the brain and muscles working. All this will mean your body fat will be used up, your hormones will be more stabilised and you will feel miles more energetic. I would even go so far as to say that your frame of mind will become much more positive.

'The hardest part is actually taking that first step to change . . . does it mean I'll never have a chocolate Hobnob ever again?'

Yes, change takes effort, but once you've started, you won't want to look back. In the next chapter I'm going to show you how to keep wanting that change and how to keep tabs on your fat-loss progress. Seeing change happen is vital to your staying power. And then you can decide whether you still need that biscuit.

'Love the eating "rules". They don't feel like rules and they gave me a real sense of freedom to cut out all the unnecessary snacking and temptation. I really love food and on this plan I didn't feel deprived once. I've had many admiring looks at my lunches as my work colleagues tuck into boring sandwiches or carb-loaded stodge.'

K.B., Devon

Chapter 6

FACING CHANGE & MONITORING YOUR PROGRESS

Somebody terribly profound once said this:

'If you want to change, you must do something differently.'

Not exactly rocket science, but whoever it was is dead right. We can sit around moaning that our clothes are tight, our ankles are swollen, that bread makes us bloated and we feel sluggish, dull and tetchy. Or we can have a go at doing something about it.

Change is daunting, isn't it? It takes effort. Nerves, even. Sometimes, we'd rather nestle back into the comfortably familiar than dip our toe into new experiences. I know I would.

But I'm telling you this. There is a whole different state of health and wellness out there and I am very keen to show it to you. The 21 Day Blast plan is going to give you the tools to lose some body fat, become stronger and more confident and inject some energy into your mental and physical wellbeing. It's about being fitter without being a slave to your workout gear and it's about being in control.

Hundreds around the world have Blast-ed their way through 21 days and are now keeping many of the plan's eating principles going in their daily lives. Which means they are continuing to get into shape. It doesn't stop at 21 days. Once you get started you'll see just what I mean. It's about being in control of what you eat . . . and eventually who you are.

'I am one of your online Blaster-ettes and I wanted to drop you a quick message. I have been pleasantly surprised at how much I am enjoying Blast. I fully expected to put on weight as I am eating better than I have in a long time. But I jumped on the scales today (sorry!) and I have lost 6lb. I'm a believer, that's for sure.'

J.P., Birmingham

See how she apologises for weighing? You'll understand why in point 5 on page 69.

Onwards . . . This next bit is about what you should do before you start the Blast plan. It's about finding your starting point and monitoring your progress because when we know it's working, we're more likely to keep going.

1. FIRST . . . IDENTIFY YOUR GOALS

Declaring, 'I want to lose some fat' is good. Saying, 'I want to be a size 12 again' or 'I want to get into those trousers that have been too tight for three years' is better, because these statements are more measurable and less vague. Other possibles are:

'I want to start doing regular exercise, but not something that is going to take over my life.'

'I want to get rid of the wind, my permanent bloating and I don't want my clothes to dig in any more.'

'I want to start my days refreshed and positive, not bleary and dreary.'

'I want to ditch temporary dieting. I want to eat in a sustainable way and get a body I'm proud of.'

'I want to be a clothes size smaller and save up for a whole new wardrobe.'

'I want someone to say, "Wow, you look amazing".'

'Some bad habits are getting the better of me; to be honest I've been using food as a crutch and I want it to stop. I can't remember the last time I was actually hungry.'

'Alcohol has become a habit. I want it to become something I savour.'

Whatever your goals, hold them in your head as you progress through this book.

2. NEXT, WRITE STUFF DOWN

I'm a great believer in getting it out of your head and on to a page. Whether you're a pen and paper, parchment and quill, finger and phone person, keep a note of how you feel, what food you eat, when you do your exercise. Write everything down. Don't be tempted to think, Oh those 10 almonds don't count. Yes they do. They count as your snack. Mindless nibbling is not going to get you into shape.

Keep a mood diary too, as well as the food diary. It's about paying closer attention to how you

feel. The first few days, your diary entry might look like this:

'Day 3, ready to sell the children for a packet of biscuits.'

Later, it might be:

'Day 5, trousers loose, great night's sleep, feeling really rather groovy.'

You'll find it very interesting reading at the end of the 21 days!

3. MEASURE!

Get a flexible tape measure (those metal DIY ones are a bit painful) and measure the parts of your body as shown in the diagram. Make a note of those measurements, then you will take them again at the end of the 21 days. Because there's nothing like being able to say proudly and with attitude, 'I've lost 9½ inches all over'.

A) Chest: Across the widest part, probably across the nipples. Women should measure with a bra on (for uplift!) but wear the same bra to re-measure later.

B) Underneath chest: Right underneath the breasts, across the top of the ribcage. A good way to determine the disappearance of back fat!

C) Tummy 1: At the smallest part, round the waist.

D) Tummy 2: Choose another part of your abdomen where you hold fat – it might be through your navel, it might be slightly higher or lower. If there is more than one, measure them all.

E) Hips: Wrap the tape measure over the largest part of your bottom.

F) Top of thigh: The fleshiest bit. You might want to earmark a freckle or something so you know where to measure next time.

G) Top of arm: Ditto the freckle.

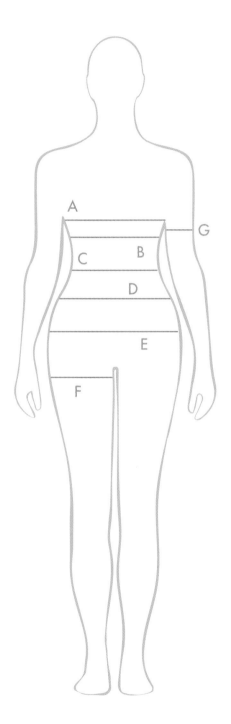

4. STRIP OFF & TAKE PHOTOGRAPHS

Look, I know it sounds like purgatory, but, really, a close encounter with one's own flesh (wobble) is the best policy. You are investing effort and time into this and this is where it will show. So get your kit off and either photograph yourself in the mirror or ask a (very good) friend to do it.

a) Take a close-up shot of your face in good light with no make-up because the tone of your skin will improve, too, as well as the actual shape of your face.

b) Take pictures of yourself in some close-fitting clothes, possibly your underwear, or even nothing at all. Front, side and rear. Tuck them away and forget about them. There will be a bit of your body that you will fixate on, we all do (I have a whole list), but unfortunately we cannot choose where the fat comes off first. It *will* come off, so just relax and focus on following the plan.

FRONT SHOT

SIDE SHOT

REAR SHOT

5. A WORD ABOUT WEIGHING: DON'T!

People always want to gauge progress by weighing, but really and truly this isn't the best way. Getting into proper shape (and by that we mean focusing on the inside as well as the outside) means we want to get smaller. We're trying to reduce in size; we're not here to get lighter. It might take a bit of hard thinking to get your head around this.

Let's look at it this way. If you have a waist currently measuring, say, 34 inches, your goal might be to shrink it to 31 inches.

So by eating right, your fat is freed from your fat cells and able to be used up. At the same time, you're exercising your muscles (see Chapter 9), which makes them firmer, stronger and tighter so they occupy a smaller space on your body. As they become denser, they may weigh more. The fat goes, but the muscle gets heavier (not bigger), so the improvement to your body visually won't necessarily be shown on the scales. But it will be in the mirror.

What happens next is, because those trousers now fit you and bits of you are firmer and tighter, you feel utterly epic and awesome. You think to yourself:

I bet I've lost at least half a stone.

So you step on. And it's one pound. One measly pound.

Then, before you know it, your motivation and resolve are spiralling downwards, your confidence is dented and your spirit is crushed.

You chuck it all in and sink your teeth into something you shouldn't – cakes, pizza, a nearby arm.

So, measure your progress and success by how you look and how things fit but not by how heavy you are. But I can say this until I'm blue in the face. People – including the Blast community – will still weigh and I will have to suck that up, as long as people realise how little weight change signifies and that it doesn't prove a hiccup in their progress. Hence some of the testimonials in this book declare joy at weight lost as well as inches dropped. It's a mindset thing. If you absolutely have to weigh, then do it once at the beginning and once at the end. A much better gauge is by photographing (see point 4) or simply by the fit of your clothes.

So we're all revved up and ready to start work. In the next chapter I'm going to outline some possible hurdles and tell you how to jump over them.

> 'I have lost over 10 inches since starting Blast, but only 2lb. I just don't bother with the scales any more. Honestly, stick with the tape measure – it's the outline we want, not whether someone can pick us up more easily!'
>
> F.N., Dorset

Chapter 7

STRATEGIES FOR SUCCESS

As a personal trainer (and previously chubby person) I am fully versed in the workings of the modern woman's mind, especially those who want to get into shape. I know the dodges, the excuses, the obstacles, the way we like to blame something else. I also know the yearning for change, the joys and the massive sense of achievement that comes with a bit of focus and discipline.

So I'm going to give you a heads-up on some feelings you might encounter and some experiences you might face. That way, there will be no surprises to take you off track – you'll be prepared for them all.

AM I HUNGRY OR IS IT SOMETHING ELSE?

Right at the start, as you tuck into your Blast way of eating and get to grips with the workouts, your motivation will be high. However, in the first few days you may start to feel something is missing. You'll wander about, kicking your heels trying to fathom it out.

> 'It's Day 4 and I had my Blast breakfast three hours ago. I'm not hungry. This is weird. I haven't succumbed to the office biscuits yet; in fact I can't think why I did before.'
>
> S.B., Surrey

You open the fridge door; shut it again. You're not hungry, so it can't be that. What IS it? You just can't put your finger on it.

Well, it's exactly that. It's all because you're not actually hungry. Nothing is missing. Nothing at all. The only thing that's missing is something sweet. But your body isn't crying out for it because your stomach isn't rumbling. It's your head saying you need that sweet fix. A metaphorical finger is tapping you on the shoulder reminding you that it's biscuit time, because that's what you always do.

You'll find there are expanses of time where your hunger is twiddling its thumbs and you won't need to fill the gap between breakfast and lunch. That might be a new concept to get your head around, but it's a very good one. Push the biscuits away. Someone else can fill their fat cells.

If you eat according to the Blast rules, then you'll be minimising hormone fluctuations (that insulin rush) and you won't find yourself feeling edgy or hungry, so there will be no reason to go hunting for a snack. Keep a note of this in your mood diary (see page 66). It might look something like this:

'Paced up and down almost feeling annoyed that I wasn't hungry. I wanted a sugar fix, but only out of habit.'

You may become a little tetchy because snacking is what you do – and now you can't do it or have little need for it. It's both weird and revealing! Read on . . .

BOREDOM & COMFORT EATING

Sometimes we snack for the sake of it and it has absolutely nothing to do with hunger; it's more about us being cross or frustrated about something. We feed our mood, rather than our body and it's often with alcohol or something sweet. I don't think anyone ever went on the hunt for a slice of chicken to appease an emotion.

'I've woken up with a black cloud hanging over me.'

'My son failed his maths test . . . again.'

'That meeting at work didn't quite go as I'd planned.'

'That guy I've got my eye on still hasn't texted back.'

'My partner and I aren't seeing eye to eye at the moment.'

We can find umpteen reasons why we should stick another biscuit in our mouths. The sweetness on our tongue wraps the whole of us in cashmere-like comfort and tells us everything will be OK, and of course it's impossible to stop at one. If you know that in advance, then hide those temptations or don't buy them in the first place. Simply tell yourself that these foods are negatives. They create a negative mood and upset the harmony you are trying to create, both in body and mind.

The craving for these mood foods won't last long and they actually will help you work out whether you are really hungry . . . or 'hangry'. If it persists, have a small handful of nuts (see page 60 for exactly how many!), because that's protein and fat but no sugar, and then do a little dance. Yes, you're in control.

Here endeth that sermon. On to another . . .

'It's a normal family evening and the TV is on and I would usually have got through half a bottle of Merlot by now. Feeling kind of perky with my strange herbal tea. Headache has gone and I have energy. I feel good, really good.'

T.B., Hampshire

THE EFFECTS OF SUGAR WITHDRAWAL

For the first couple of days you might have the mother of all headaches. A vice around your head and a knot in your stomach. This is simply your body craving sugar, more caffeine, alcohol, anything it was used to and which is now out of bounds. It will also be your brain saying this:

'This book . . . and that Deadman woman . . . say I can't have it. Which makes me want it all the more.'

Funny thing, human nature.

It's all perfectly normal and you can think of it as the old you taking a hike and the determined new you settling into position. It might last for a couple of days; you'll be a bit grumpy and crotchety but don't let it weaken your resolve. Provide your friends and family with suitable armour and tell them not to talk to you unless absolutely necessary. Drink lots of fluid, stick with it and you'll come out shining, I promise.

'Day 16. I'm very happy today. I took a photo and compared it with me two weeks ago and I've definitely got more muscle definition in my arms and tum. Two inches off my waist! Also, my appetite has definitely decreased. My husband kept waving Celebrations chocs and Pringles under my nose at the cinema last night and I just didn't bat an eyelid. Nada. No urge whatsoever. How very liberating!'

J.C., Edinburgh

YAWWWWN . . .

Before the energetic high kicks in, you may feel strangely tired, like you're dragging yourself through the day. It's simply your body adapting to the changes. This won't last, but again it will be fluids and good, nourishing Blast food that will get you through and out the other side, as well as the prospect of seeing some changes in your body. Don't overthink it. Just do it.

THE LURE OF ALCOHOL

Change means putting a stop to old habits. If the nightly glass or three of wine is something you think needs addressing, then brilliant, good for you. Swapping from nightly to weekend drinking will, without doubt, improve your health now (and your prospects for the future), your energy levels and your body shape. This 21-day period of going without will be tough; I won't pretend it isn't. Alcohol does, after all, numb the negatives of life. This is going to be one of your biggest hurdles and there's not only your own discipline to deal with, there's the attitude of your friends, too:

'Oh go on, one won't hurt. What d'you mean, you're not drinking? Oh, that's just great . . . spoil all our fun, why don't you?'

Or

'Come on, you're much more fun when you've had a drink, just a teensy little gin. It's only about 75 calories with a slimline tonic . . . Who's to know?'

YOU'LL know.

And it's not about the number of calories. It's about staying true to something that you have set your mind on.

You're a grown-up; you can do exactly as you please. You could toss this book (and your powers of restraint) aside and join them. You could also just ignore it and stay focused. Just because you're not joining them in their froth and fizz, doesn't mean you've suddenly had a personality transplant. You can still be fun, do the banter thing, but you sure as hell aren't going to be persuaded out of something you're working hard for. I'm right, aren't I? Which leads us on to . . .

'In front of me, my husband has drunk a bottle of beer and is now eating biscuits. I'm not even tempted. That's quite a shift in my mental attitude.'

M.T., London

THOSE WHO WANT TO BRING YOU DOWN

This is rare and they are unlikely to be true friends. Identify them and give them a wide berth. Keep your hopes, aspirations and stories of sore thighs and clothes that now fit to yourself. It's less pressure for you and less ammunition for them. There will always be the helpful soul who asks questions . . .

Friend: 'How's your diet going? You look like you've lost tons of weight.'

You: 'It's only Day 2 and it's not a diet.'

Friend: 'Ooh, you don't want to be getting too thin. Gaunt and bony isn't an attractive look.'

This is code for: 'I don't want you succeeding at something I'm not part of.'

COPING WITH PLANNED DAYS/NIGHTS OUT

Applying yourself to a different way of eating and avoiding alcohol doesn't mean your social life has to shut down. Keep your friends but keep your motivation too. Whatever the occasion, any restaurant can provide a Blast-friendly meal of a cut of protein (chicken, fish, steak or vegetarian equivalent) and a pile of vegetables, without being drenched in a suspicious sweet sauce. Offer to be their driver for the evening, then sip your mineral water with pride (garnished with mint and a sprinkling of smug). You avoid the peer pressure and they will be eternally grateful.

COPING WITH YOUR PARTNER EATING YOUR SHARE OF THE SATURDAY-NIGHT CHOCOLATE

A swift kick somewhere painful.

BLAMING FOOD FOR EVERYTHING

When you're feeling utterly fed up (your meeting didn't go well, someone at work is being difficult, everything is going wrong at home) then the first thing you will want to do is blame Blast.

That is the time to jot down notes in your mood diary. You may be alarmed at how much you think about food to soothe issues other than hunger.

STAYING POSITIVE, UPBEAT & WANTING SUCCESS

None of this is about being a size 8. It's about being a trimmer version of you and about discovering how this way of eating will affect the harmony of your gut. It's about losing inches, finding energy and learning mindfulness (see opposite). It's not about meandering through life becoming a victim of whatever it throws at us. It's about using your body's new-found strength to deal with the pitfalls that will undoubtedly lie in your way.

Through my years as a personal trainer and through running the 21 Day Blast I have seen so many women unhappy with their lot, nibbling on crispbreads, with dwindling metabolisms and fading strength, and hoping desperately that a new (and smaller) version of themselves

will be born. All that happens is the body slows down and that fat isn't burnt. Their muscle is wasted away (because the body wants to hold on to the fat for fear of going hungry) and they lose strength and tone. This attracts illness, weakness and a negative self-attitude.

So they eat even less, get murderously hungry then chuck it all in and binge on the wrong foods. At which point the body thinks, Yes, yes, yes! Food at last! It grabs those calories and stuffs them into the fat cells for later. It's a vicious cycle. A lose-lose . . .

Blast is going to help us break those cycles. Yes, in just 21 days.

MINDFULNESS . . . WILL IT HELP?

It's a bit of a buzzword at the moment and it can mean a lot of different things depending on who you listen to. For the purposes of our Blast project, let's look at it like this: mindfulness is the basic human ability to be fully present in the moment, aware of where we are and what we're doing, and not overly reactive or overwhelmed by what's going on around us.

'Have you gone mad? How have I got time to be fully present in my own moment when I've a report to write, my son's homework to check, the dishwasher has bust and now the peas are boiling over!'

I don't mean ignore your family; I don't even mean sit and meditate. I just mean pay attention to your thoughts and feelings and actions. To what is happening to you. Let's take eating for example. How often do you eat a snack, take one bite and then moments later you look down and see an empty packet? You can't actually remember chomping and chewing it. We are all brilliant at multitasking and our attention dances from one thing to the next far too quickly. I'm saying try and think about you, about what you're eating, how your mood changes. Give yourself time. I'm not asking you to become selfish, just a bit more self-aware.

GETTING SUGAR SAVVY

Insulin is produced in response to eating carbohydrates – whether they are the starchy (complex carbs) or the more sugary form (simple carbs). We are trying to minimise insulin production because the more glucose that is produced from the carbs we eat, the more body fat we store – which is the opposite of what we want.

Sugar can be found in some foods where we least expect it. So we need to get smart and stay on the lookout. Anything that says 99% fat free or 0% fat is usually a danger zone. The fat will have been replaced by sugar to give it flavour. This means, when you're looking at food labels, be sure to check out the 'of which sugars' content.

Take yoghurt, for example: there is a massive nutritional difference among the brands offered. See Yoghurt 1, on the next page, which is low in sugar but high in protein – perfect for satiety. However, Yoghurt 2 has double the sugar but less protein.

Yoghurt 1

Typical values	per 100g
Energy	230kJ / 54kcal
Carbohydrate	3.0g
of which sugars	3.0g
Protein	10.3g

Yoghurt 2

Typical values	Per 100g
Energy	255kJ / 60kcal
Carbohydrate	8.7g
of which sugars	8.7g
Protein	6.1g

So when choosing non-sweet products (and by this I mean products that you wouldn't expect to contain sugar – such as savoury goods, sauces, etc.) try to stick to products that have no more than 4g of sugar per 100g, less if possible.

(Note that some of our Anytime foods are actually high in carbohydrate, for example chickpeas, lentils, cannellini beans. But their sugar content is very, very low and I include them because they are a good source of protein, particularly for vegetarians and vegans.)

THE FOOD-LABEL TRAPS

Food manufacturers are cunning; with their packaging design and clever wording you can soon be lulled into thinking a product is 'healthy'. Take granola, for example. Next time you do your shopping, just have a look at all the cute illustrations and the natural-looking brown paper cartons. Granola . . . sounds crunchy and wholesome like Granny used to make. It will benefit our health.

The hell it will.

Obviously not all cereals are tarred with the same poisonous brush, but check out the box. The ingredients might go something like this (in this order): Oat Flakes, Sugar, Raisins, Puffed Brown Rice, Roasted Hazelnuts, Pecan Nuts, Honey, Pumpkin Seeds, Sunflower Oil.

Sugar is second on the list. It doesn't take a degree in nutrition to know that means it's the second-biggest ingredient.

Similarly, as you become wise to all things sugary, you'll start spotting clever words of enticement. Words like Harvest, Oaty, Crispy, Honey Nut, Nature's Kitchen, Naked, Skinny, Supergrain, Raw, Light, Proper, Market, Deli . . . oh, I could go on and on.

Then there's the buzzwords like Protein in big fat letters or Spelt or Whole-Grain. These may be important to know, but it doesn't necessarily make them good for us or mean they have a place on Blast. It might mean they've been drenched in sugar/honey/maple syrup/dextrose/maltose – or some other unrecognisable -ose. It's all sugar.

Obviously some words, like 'gluten-free' tell truths not veiled fibs. For those who are coeliac, it is essential to see those words emblazoned on the packet, but, again, it's possible that lack of gluten has led to lack of taste, which can only be disguised by sugar.

Most of the time during Blast you will be cooking food from scratch. However, there are bound to be times when you are running short of time and need a few shortcuts. Ready meals and processed food of any kind should be kept to an absolute minimum to avoid false flavours or a kick-start to your sweet tooth, but the following items will help out in an emergency.

- Pouches of ready-cooked rice, quinoa, lentils

- Ready-cooked chicken and fish (worth ditching the chicken skin to save any showdown with a dodgy barbecue-flavour coating)

- Frozen goods of course, such as cauliflower rice, ready-prepared butternut squash, and I am a big fan of bags of frozen berries, diced onion and peppers . . . so time-saving

- Some canned and fresh soups (do scrutinise the contents, though)

- Jars of sugar-free curry pastes (you might have to look hard, but they are out there)

- Packets of oatcakes and rice cakes. There are quinoa and lentil varieties now, too, which add to your protein intake

The next chunk of the book is given up to food prep and delicious recipes. After that we look at EXERCISE. This, my lovely friends, is going to galvanise your resolve and prove the perfect complement to Blast nutrition. YOU are going to become a fat-burning machine.

The great thing about Blast is that it lends itself very well to everyday living. That means this glorious collection of recipes will not only help you lose fat and sort out gut issues but also make your family drool. The recipes are easy and straightforward. We love food, but I don't want you to spend too much time – or brainpower – concocting extravagant nosh. So I've done it for you.

The Blast food lists in Chapter 5 give you your permitted foods for both Anytime and After Workout meals, as well as the list of non-permitted foods. This will enable you to create your shopping list.

In Chapter 8, I've written some suggestions for store-cupboard ingredients that feature in the recipes and which may be over and above what you already have in. It won't mean forking out for expensive items you've never heard of. It's more of an 'Ooooh, I never thought of that' list.

TO WRAP UP

If we weren't battling against our emotions and our hormones and the stuff that life throws at us, then this whole fat-loss malarkey would be easy. We'd all have Instagram bodies. But it's not. Most of us have families, homes and busy lives that take up our time and we have to somehow find the wherewithall to focus on ourselves. And that's what we're doing.

The results that make the whole Blast plan worth doing are these:

- Fat loss (smaller body parts and a decreased health risk)

- Increased fitness, strength and therefore a body with a higher metabolism

- Fewer digestive and gut issues, whether full-blown IBS or constipation and indigestion

- Better sleep

- Improved skin – and often hair and nails too

- More energy

- A better understanding of, and respect for, your own body and health

- Fewer mood changes associated with hormone levels

- A decreased sweet tooth

- Eczema, hay fever and fungal infections will subside and may disappear altogether

- A higher level of self-worth

You will experience some or all of these things in 21 days. You'll make new discoveries about your own body and they will, hopefully, result in you wanting to make *permanent* changes to your lifestyle. There's plenty of help with this in Chapter 12, but for now we're in for some mouth-watering inspiration, because the next chunk of the book is given over to food prep and delicious recipes and we kick off by suggesting some additions to your store cupboard.

Chapter 8

THE BLAST RECIPES

STORE-CUPBOARD/FRIDGE SUGGESTIONS

- Coconut: both the flaked and the desiccated kind

- Seeds: pumpkin, sunflower and chia seeds – now, these last little gems are worth a mention. They seem to have found their feet in recent times and edged their way to the top of the trendy ingredients chart, but I have to say with good reason. These tiny black pinhead seeds are high in omega-3 fats, contain all 20 amino acids and provide a good dose of fibre as well as some important minerals. If you're vegan, then use them as a substitute for egg in baking and cooking. Simply soak 1 tablespoon in 3 tablespoons of water and leave for about 15 minutes for them to swell up. Looks a bit like frogspawn, but works a treat

- Quinoa: a protein-packed grain – high in the amino acid lysine

- Buckwheat: flour and groats (funny rock-hard little nuggets)

- Gram flour: also called chickpea flour

- Cacao powder: unlike cocoa powder, this is the purest form of chocolate and we use a smidgen of this in a few of the recipes. It oozes antioxidants

- Tofu: a soft white block made from soy bean curd, with a very mild flavour

- Tempeh: also from bean curd but denser, more chewy and with a distinct flavour

- Pulses and beans: red lentils, chickpeas, cannellini beans, black beans, kidney beans, butter beans – high in protein, very filling

- Wheat-free pasta: there are varieties made from non-wheat grains such as buckwheat and rice, as well as versions made out of beans and pulses. Worth exploring if you are a pasta fan

- Nuts: walnuts, almonds, cashews . . . any roasted or natural, just not covered in chocolate or with any other suspect coating (for a nudge about portion sizes, see page 60). Flaked and ground almonds are useful too

- Hummus: any no-sugar variety (although better to make your own)

- Tahini paste: this appears in some of the recipes; it's a lovely goo made from sesame seeds

- Almond or peanut butter: choose the no-sugar and no-palm-oil varieties – you'll need your powers of restraint

- Sauces: fish sauce, soy sauce (or tamari, which is wheat-free)

- Apple cider vinegar: this is a marvellous addition to your kitchen shelf. It's great for using in salad dressings as its acetic-acid content helps promote our good gut bacteria. It helps the absorption of nutrients from our food as well as easing blood-sugar spikes after eating. It also helps lower blood pressure and is an aid to treating acid reflux. I've used it in baking to make After Workout muffins rise (see the Snacks section, page 210) and as if that weren't enough, it also naturally whitens your teeth and makes your hair shine if applied directly and mixed with water. Be sure to buy a raw, unfiltered

version with 'the mother', which contains the enzymes and gut-friendly bacteria responsible for most of the health benefits

- Salad vinegars: includes balsamic, to give a boost to your greenery, when added to a little oil

- Stock: any very-low or no-sugar varieties

- Dairy-free milk: unsweetened almond, coconut, rice, hemp, soya varieties

- Oils: coconut oil (hard stuff in a jar), olive oil, rapeseed oil, plus walnut or avocado oil if you want something fancy for careful drizzling

- Mustard: all types

- Herbs and spices: dried, fresh or frozen, especially garlic, ginger, mint, basil, cumin, coriander, ground cardamom, turmeric, cinnamon, smoked paprika

- Bottled water: tap water is fine, too, but some sparkling fizz in a glass with a tall stem can feel more special . . . OK, not as special as Prosecco

- Lemons and limes: for drinks and cooking

- Herbal teas: lose yourself in the caffeine-free drinks aisle

- Protein powder: there are a number of sugar-free and dairy-free brands available. Some of them make you want to gag. My personal preference is soy protein powder. You may have also come across spirulina, which is hailed as a superfood. It's made from green algae (I'm not selling it well, am I?) and is absolutely stuffed full of vitamins, minerals and antioxidants, but you'll need a strong stomach. Think pond water. Concentrated

THE BLAST RECIPES

On now to the Recipes section, which is divided into:

- Breakfasts & brunches

- Light meals, soups & salads

- Hearty meals

- Sides, dips & relishes

- Snacks

Each section is separated out into Anytime and After Workout recipes. The After Workout meals include a portion of carbohydrate, so be sure to plan your meals according to when you're doing your workout and eat afterwards.

I've also included plenty of what I call 'one-liners'. These are at-a-glance simple ideas that are about food assembly rather than cooking and you can knock them up in no time. You don't have to follow recipes at all if you don't want to, so these are useful ideas for making up your own dishes.

Remember, the Blast guidelines (Chapter 5) state that you must make Anytime food choices for all your meals, except the meal that follows a workout, which must be an After Workout meal because that will contain starchy carbohydrate.

The recipe collection is full of loveliness, but it is intended as inspiration – it's not meant to be prescriptive. When you've grasped the Blast rules, you may just want to do your own thing and adapt your own repertoire of recipes that you know work for you and your family.

BREAKFASTS & BRUNCHES

Try and think of breakfast as less of a meal poured out of a cereal box but something much more fortifying! If you're planning on doing your exercise later on in the day, then your breakfast choices will be from the Anytime lists.

If you prefer an early workout, you can refuel from the After Workout section. Try a slice of the Courgette Bread toasted with a couple of fried eggs – you won't even think about food till lunch.

GRAIN-FREE GRANOLA

Makes 16 servings, each 2 heaped tablespoons
Calories per serving 238 | Protein per serving 4.7g

This is my version of a 'no cereal' granola (there's a lovely buckwheat After Workout granola on page 114, too). Two heaped tablespoons with some lovely thick Greek yoghurt is the recommended portion size because it's extremely filling and also quite calorie-dense. It will keep in an airtight container for a couple of weeks.

250g shredded coconut flakes

50g sunflower seeds

50g pumpkin seeds

100g chopped roasted hazelnuts (skin off, preferably)

100g chopped almonds

1 tsp ground cinnamon

1 tsp ground ginger

50g coconut oil, melted

Preheat the oven to 180°C/160°C Fan/Gas 4.

Combine all the dry ingredients in a bowl, mixing well.

Pour over the melted oil and again mix well.

Grease and line a shallow baking tray and pour over the mixture, levelling it out with your hands.

Bake in the oven on the middle shelf for 20–25 minutes. Stir the contents twice during that time so the crispiness becomes even and the surface doesn't burn.

Transfer to an airtight container when cool . . . without nibbling. Tricky.

BROCCOLI and SALMON FRITTATA

Serves 4–6 | Calories per serving 212 | Protein per serving 15g

What I love about this is a) it has broccoli (my favourite ultimate superfood) and b) you can cut it up and freeze it into the perfect breakfast-sized portions. Anything time-saving, we're up for!

1 tbsp coconut oil or rapeseed oil

1 red onion, sliced

1 red pepper, deseeded and sliced

2 garlic cloves, sliced

150g broccoli florets

handful of fresh or frozen garden peas

200g salmon fillet, cut into large chunks

7 medium eggs

handful of fresh chives, snipped

salt and freshly ground black pepper

Heat half the coconut or rapeseed oil in a large frying pan with a heatproof handle and sauté the onion, pepper, garlic and broccoli for 6–8 minutes.

Add the peas and salmon, and cook for another 2 minutes.

Beat the eggs in a large bowl and add the snipped chives and seasoning.

Tip the sautéed vegetables and salmon into the egg mixture and stir well.

Heat the remaining coconut or rapeseed oil in the pan and pour in the frittata mixture. Cook over a medium–low heat for 18–20 minutes, or until the frittata appears to be set (you can prise the edge away slightly with a palette knife to check).

Preheat the grill to hot and place the pan under. Cook the top of the frittata until it is golden brown.

To remove the frittata from the pan, place your palette knife underneath to ease it away from any sticking place and then place a plate over the top (cue drum rolling) and flip it over quickly . . . when no one is looking. Cut into wedges and serve.

CAULIFLOWER HASH BROWNS

Serves 2 | Calories per serving 123 (with 75g smoked salmon, 258)
Protein per serving 7.5g (with 75g smoked salmon, 25.5g)

These sound a faff, but they're really not. Simple and quick to knock up, they make a tasty breakfast served with grilled bacon and tomatoes, or smoked salmon, yoghurt and a squirt of lemon.

300g cauliflower, leaves removed

2 medium eggs

2 spring onions, trimmed and finely chopped

¼ tsp ground turmeric

½ tsp coconut oil or olive oil

salt and freshly ground black pepper

Break the cauliflower into florets, put into a blender and process until completely broken down into a rice-like consistency. If it's still a bit knobbly, it won't matter.

Whisk the eggs in a large bowl, then add the cauliflower, spring onions, turmeric and seasoning.

Heat the oil in a large frying pan and spoon all the egg mixture in 4 large spoonfuls into the pan.

Cook over a medium heat for 4–5 minutes until golden underneath, then carefully turn over and cook for a further 3–4 minutes.

Serve accompanied by your favourite protein.

TOFU MUSHROOM SCRAMBLE

Serves 2 | Calories per serving 220 | Protein per serving 14.8g

You can of course add any other herbs and spices you like to this dish, but I didn't want to overdo it, seeing as it is only breakfast. This is packed with goodness – even if you're a staunch meat eater, give it a try.

250g firm tofu, drained and cut into cubes

2 tsp tamari or soy sauce

1 garlic clove, crushed

1 tbsp olive oil

1 small leek, trimmed and thinly sliced

150g mushrooms, sliced

100g cherry tomatoes on the vine

50g spinach leaves

salt and freshly ground black pepper

Place the tofu in a non-metallic bowl and sprinkle with the tamari or soy and garlic. Toss to coat with the flavours.

Heat the oil in a frying pan and sauté the leek and mushrooms for 4–5 minutes.

Meanwhile, preheat the grill to hot and grill the cherry tomatoes on the vine until they're just starting to burst.

Add the marinated tofu to the frying pan and with a fork, break up the cubes by lightly mashing them into the pan.

Stir the spinach into the pan and cook until just wilted. Season.

Divide the tofu scramble between two warmed plates and top with the grilled cherry tomatoes to serve.

THE BLAST SMOOTHIE

Serves 1 | Calories 225 | Protein 5g

If you aren't very good at having breakfast but feel you want something to kick-start your energy, then a smoothie might be just the thing. There are lots of possible variants, but this recipe is a good place to start. Add a spoonful of hemp protein powder for a bigger protein kick. Vitamins, minerals, good fats; away you go!

300ml unsweetened
coconut milk

½ small avocado, peeled

1 tbsp frozen (or fresh)
blueberries

large handful of
spinach leaves

1 tsp peanut butter

Place all the ingredients in a blender and whizz until frothy and a weird purple colour. It tastes glorious. I promise.

MEXICAN BEAN BREAKFAST BOWL

Serves 2 | Calories per serving 406 | Protein per serving 17.5g

No more canned baked beans on a slimy bit of bread for us. Oh no! We're going to double up on nutrients with this one. This also makes a perfect lunch.

2 tsp olive oil

½ red pepper, deseeded and diced

½ tsp smoked paprika

400g can cannellini beans, drained and rinsed

25g sweetcorn (canned or frozen is fine)

227g can chopped tomatoes

small handful of spinach leaves

8 thin slices of chorizo

1 avocado, peeled, stoned and sliced

To serve

1 tsp sunflower seeds, toasted

1 tsp sesame seeds, toasted

squeeze of lime juice

Heat the oil in a large pan and sauté the pepper for 2–3 minutes. Add the smoked paprika and cook for 1 more minute.

Stir in the cannellini beans, sweetcorn and tomatoes, and bring to a simmer. Cook for 4–5 minutes.

Divide the spinach between two bowls then top with the bean mixture, chorizo and avocado slices.

Serve with a sprinkle of toasted seeds and a squeeze of lime juice.

NUT and BERRY BREAKFAST JAR

Serves 1 | Calories 414 | Protein 23.4g

This gorgeous breakfast involves a bit more prepping, but, once done, it's compulsory to eat it out of a tall fancy glass or jar . . . and in front of others. You'll be the envy of them all with their sad piece of toast!

100g raspberries

2 tsp chia seeds

175g Greek yoghurt

60g strawberries, hulled and sliced

10g pecan nuts, chopped

10g Brazil nuts, chopped

10g pistachio nuts, chopped

1 tsp cacao powder

mint leaves, to garnish (optional)

Place the raspberries and chia seeds in a small blender and blend to a paste. Leave to stand for 2 minutes to thicken slightly.

Spoon half the yoghurt into a jar then top with the strawberry slices, keeping a few for the top.

Spoon over the raspberry mixture then top with the remaining yoghurt.

Place the chopped nuts in a small frying pan and cook over a medium heat, making sure they don't burn. Remove from the heat and stir in the cacao powder.

Spoon the cacao-coated nuts on top of the yoghurt and finish with the remaining strawberry slices. Either serve immediately with mint leaves, if you like, or chill in the fridge until required.

SMOKED HADDOCK OMELETTE

Serves 1 | Calories 360 | Protein 35.6g

Just look at the protein this dish delivers! A fortifying breakfast if ever there was one.

80g smoked haddock fillet

300ml unsweetened non-dairy milk

3 medium eggs, beaten

½ tbsp olive oil

1 tbsp chopped flatleaf parsley

salt and freshly ground black pepper

Place the haddock and milk in a small pan and bring to a simmer. Cover and cook for 5–6 minutes until the fish is just cooked through. Lift the fish out of the pan and gently break into large flakes, retaining the milk.

Whisk together the eggs and 1 tablespoon of the milk in which the fish was cooked. Season.

Heat the olive oil in a frying pan and pour in the egg mixture. Cook over a medium heat, moving the eggs around until they are nearly cooked.

Sprinkle the flaked fish and half of the chopped parsley over the omelette, then fold the omelette in half and slide on to a warmed plate. Sprinkle over the remaining parsley to serve.

BREAKFAST ONE-LINERS

- Two good-quality gluten-free sausages, with some grilled tomatoes and mushrooms

- Two poached eggs with wilted spinach

- Ratatouille with smoked haddock

- Two rashers of grilled back bacon, one fried egg, a handful of mushrooms and two tomatoes sautéed in a teaspoon of oil . . . Yes, a fry-up!

- Two boiled eggs and asparagus soldiers

- Smoked salmon slices filled with yoghurt, dill and a squeeze of lemon

- Turkey steak, sautéed with a spoon of diced chorizo, spinach and tomatoes (talk about protein-packed!)

- 200g Greek yoghurt, a handful of your favourite berries and 10–15 almonds

- Sweetcorn fritters with poached egg: about 50g sweetcorn mixed with 2 eggs (or egg white) and chopped spring onion, then sautéed in dollops. Eat as they are or serve with a rasher of bacon or a small fillet of smoked fish

- Bombay-spiced omelette: add chopped onion and curry powder to your eggs! And some leftover vegetables too

SWEET POTATO ROSTI

Serves 2 | Calories per serving 211 (plus one egg and one rasher of bacon, 326)
Protein per serving 2.8g (13.3g)

*These are really lovely, especially as a weekend post-sweat treat. Topped with a
runny poached egg and a slice of bacon, they're a great start to the day.*

325g sweet
potato, peeled

1 tbsp olive oil

½ red onion, thinly sliced

salt and freshly ground
black pepper

Grate the sweet potatoes into a large bowl. Using your hands,
squeeze the grated potato over a bowl or sink, to get rid of as
much liquid as possible.

Heat half the olive oil in a frying pan and sauté the onion for
2–3 minutes until soft.

Add the onion to the sweet potato, mix together and season well.

Heat the remaining olive oil in the same frying pan. Using your
hands again, squeeze together a ball of the sweet potato mixture,
then flatten into a rosti shape and add to the pan. Repeat with the
remaining mixture, to make four rosti.

Cook over a medium heat for 6–8 minutes until the bottom is
golden and the shape holds together. Gently flip the rosti over and
cook for 5–6 minutes on the other side. Press down with a spatula
from time to time, to ensure they are cooking all the way through.

Serve hot, topped with crispy bacon and a poached egg if wished.

BUCKWHEAT-BERRY BREAKFAST MUFFINS

Makes 12 | Calories per muffin 105 | Protein per muffin 4.1g

There are lots of varieties of frozen berries in the supermarkets these days. This recipe uses strawberries and blueberries, but it works just as well with any of your favourite berries, either fresh or frozen. Two of these with a bowl of high-protein Greek yoghurt make a lovely After Workout breakfast. Almost like trifle, it's food for the soul!

145g buckwheat flour

55g ground almonds

25g rolled oats

1 tsp baking powder

1 tsp ground cinnamon

pinch of salt

1 banana, peeled
(about 100g)

150ml unsweetened
non-dairy milk
(I used almond)

1 tbsp Greek yoghurt

2 medium eggs

75g blueberries

75g strawberries, hulled
and chopped

Preheat the oven to 200°C/180°C Fan/Gas 6. Line a 12-hole muffin tray with paper cases.

Place the flour, ground almonds, oats, baking powder, cinnamon and salt in a large bowl.

Mash the banana in a smaller bowl.

Whisk together the milk, yoghurt and eggs in a separate bowl and then stir in the banana.

Pour the egg and banana mixture into the dry ingredients and mix together gently.

Add the berries and stir until well combined.

Spoon into the muffin cases and bake for 17–20 minutes, or until golden.

Cool on a wire rack. And hide from the children.

KEDGEREE

Serves 4 | Calories per serving 242 | Protein per serving 20.5g

This works well for a weekend breakfast when you might have more time (and I quite like it for lunch if I've done my workout a bit later). Rice, fish and eggs with herbs are a winning combination.

1 tbsp coconut oil
or olive oil

1 large onion, chopped

1 tsp ground coriander

1 tsp ground turmeric

2 tsp curry powder

250g basmati rice, rinsed

60g asparagus tips

300g salmon fillet, cut
into bite-size pieces

2 medium eggs

handful of chopped
flatleaf parsley

handful of
chopped coriander

salt and freshly ground
black pepper

Heat the oil in a large heavy-based pan and sauté the onion for 4–5 minutes until softened.

Stir in the spices and cook for another minute.

Add the rice and asparagus, and stir well to coat with the spices. Pour in 600ml water, stir then bring to the boil. Reduce to a simmer, cover and cook for 5 minutes.

Add the salmon, cover and cook for a further minute then remove from the heat and leave to stand, still covered, for 8–10 minutes.

Meanwhile, boil the eggs in a pan of boiling water for 6–7 minutes. Peel the shells from the eggs and cut into quarters.

Gently mix the eggs and herbs into the kedgeree, season to taste and serve immediately, because the aroma will drive you insane.

BUCKWHEAT GALETTES

Serves 2 | Calories per serving (2 pancakes) 257 | Protein per serving 12.7g

These pancakes are just as good for lunch as they are for breakfast. So any left over you could save for tomorrow for an After Workout lunch stuffed with prawns, chicken, tuna or that lovely Red Lentil and Coriander Relish in the Sides, Dips & Relishes section on page 194 – we're thinking outside the breakfast box, remember.

100g buckwheat flour

pinch of salt

1 large egg

300ml unsweetened coconut or almond milk (I like a mix)

smidgen of coconut oil, for frying each pancake

Sweet or savoury toppings or fillings

Berries and yoghurt

Hummus and rocket

Tofu and peppers

Avocado, basil and tomatoes

Mix the flour and salt together in a bowl.

In a jug mix the egg and the milk until combined.

Pour half the milk and egg into the flour mixture and stir briskly to a paste. Then add the rest of the milk, whisking as you go.

Heat a heavy-based non-stick frying pan until really hot and then add a tiny bit of coconut oil. Spoon in some of the mixture to cover the base of the pan (to make a nice thin pancake).

Each galette will take about 2–3 minutes to cook on each side. Transfer to a warm plate until they are all cooked.

Annie's Tip: *These fold up well into a foil pack, so are nicely portable if you prefer to eat on the hoof.*

COURGETTE BREAD

Makes 12 lovely dense slices | Calories per slice 156 (2 slices would do as your portion of carbs) | Protein per slice 6.5g

Yes . . . bread! This is a wonderful wheat-free replacement for bread and has been very popular with our online Blast members. It freezes well, toasts beautifully and is great with scrambled eggs or with a teaspoon of peanut butter. The grated courgettes lend a lovely moistness and the buckwheat flour makes it so filling. Be gone, spongy bread that makes you bloated.

225g buckwheat flour

225g porridge oats

1 tsp ground cinnamon

½ tsp salt

1 tsp baking powder

225g grated courgette

3 medium eggs, beaten

80ml unsweetened non-dairy milk

1 large ripe banana, mashed

Preheat the oven to 180°C/160°C Fan/Gas 4. Grease and line a loaf tin.

In a bowl mix together the buckwheat flour, oats, cinnamon, salt and baking powder.

Add the grated courgette and mix well.

In a jug, beat the eggs with the milk and add the mashed banana. Add all that to the dry ingredients.

Mix well, ensuring you include all the dry bits at the bottom of the bowl. It will be very dense and sticky, which is perfect.

Transfer the mixture to the lined tin, smooth out and bake on the middle shelf of the oven for 50–55 minutes. It should be a golden-brown colour and if you pierce it with a skewer it will be moist inside. Which is good!

Remove from the tin, leave to cool completely on a wire rack, covered with a tea towel, then cut into 12 slices and freeze.

MINI SWEET POTATO and BACON FRITTATAS

Makes 12　|　Calories per frittata 85　|　Protein per frittata 6.3g

The sweet potato here adds the refuelling carbohydrate that you will need if you've done your workout early. Two or three of these will keep you firing on all cylinders until lunchtime! They also make popular additions to children's lunchboxes.

400g sweet potato, peeled and diced

4 rashers of back bacon

2 spring onions, trimmed and thinly sliced

7 medium eggs

100ml unsweetened non-dairy milk

½ tsp smoked paprika

salt and freshly ground black pepper

Preheat the oven to 200°C/180°C Fan/Gas 6. Grease a 12-hole muffin tray.

Place the diced sweet potato in a pan and cover with water. Bring to the boil, cover and simmer for 8–10 minutes until tender.

Meanwhile, preheat the grill to hot and grill the bacon for 3–4 minutes on both sides.

Drain the sweet potato and divide among the 12 muffin holes.

Chop the bacon and sprinkle over the sweet potato, then top with the spring onions.

Beat together the eggs and milk in a large jug. Season.

Pour the egg mixture over the potato, bacon and onions, leaving a space of approximately 1cm from the top to allow for the mixture to rise.

Sprinkle over the paprika and bake for 25 minutes until puffy and golden.

OVERNIGHT OATS
4 SCRUMPTIOUS VARIATIONS

This is one of the most popular post-workout breakfasts on the Blast plan. All of them involve overnight soaking of oats . . . and that's basically it! Your breakfast is then ready to take to work or to enjoy when the children have gone to school. The recipes work best with smaller porridge oats as opposed to the bigger jumbo ones, and the addition of chia seeds makes the mixture swell up, giving it a delicious stodginess. If you want to increase the protein quota, add a spoonful of soy protein powder, in which case you might need a dash more liquid.

The variations opposite give a quantity of oats and liquid along with assorted fillings. All you need to do in all cases is measure out the ingredients, transfer to a screwtop jar and mix well. Place in the fridge overnight, then when you've done your workout, your dream breakfast is waiting for you. (Sometimes I have this as part of my lunch if I've done my workout later.)

CHOCOLATE and CHERRY CHIA

Serves 1 | Calories 353 | Protein 10.4g

A ch-ch-cheery start to the day.

60g oats

200ml almond milk

10g chia seeds (2 tsp)

½ tsp cacao powder

½ tsp ground cinnamon

10 fresh or frozen cherries (you can put straight into the mixture frozen)

APPLE and CINNAMON

Serves 1 | Calories 371 | Protein 12.5g

This could almost, almost be apple crumble.

60g oats

150ml almond milk

50g Greek yoghurt (1 heaped tbsp)

1 small apple, peeled and grated

1 tsp pumpkin seeds

½ tsp ground cinnamon

BANANA and PEANUT BUTTER

Serves 1 | Calories 380 | Protein 10.7g

This one is a little bit dangerous . . . depends if you can be trusted (unlike me) with an open jar of peanut butter in the house.

60g oats

200ml almond or rice milk

10g chia seeds

1 heaped tsp peanut butter (smooth or crunchy)

½ small banana, chopped (save the other half for the next day)

pinch of ground cinnamon (optional)

BLUEBERRY and COCONUT

Serves 1 | Calories 360 | Protein 9.7g

My daughter Emily is a teacher and this is her favourite – it gives her the perfect amount of oomph to deal with a class of 30 little ones.

60g oats

50g frozen blueberries

200ml coconut milk

1 tbsp yoghurt

1 tbsp desiccated coconut (optional)

POWER GRANOLA

Makes 12 servings | Calories per 40g serving 215 | Protein per 40g serving 5.6g

Granola, unlike porridge, has a good bit of crunch to it, but so many of the shop-bought varieties contain honey, maple syrup or some secret sugar. So I've come up with this. The buckwheat groats give it a wonderful crispness. It is very softly sweetened with apple purée (takes 10 minutes to make your own and you can freeze it in ice-cube trays). A small bowl of this with Greek yoghurt or almond milk and a few berries will keep you going for hours. The groats shouldn't need pre-soaking if you buy the pale golden variety. If you want to be sure, just pop them in water for a couple of hours and then drain and pat dry.

100g raw buckwheat groats

250g jumbo rolled oats (use the big ones, the small porridge-y ones won't cut it)

2 tsp ground cinnamon

¼ teaspoon grated nutmeg

30g coconut flakes

30g pumpkin seeds

20g sesame seeds

½ tsp salt

50g cashew nuts

50g hazelnuts

15g coconut oil, melted

4 tbsp apple purée (about 150g)

Preheat the oven to 200°C/180°C Fan/Gas 6 and line a large baking tray with baking parchment.

Combine the buckwheat and oats in a bowl with the cinnamon, nutmeg, coconut flakes, seeds and salt. Mix well.

Put the nuts in a dry frying pan and roast for about 2–3 minutes (no oil) to bring out their flavour. It's tempting to skip this bit but it really does boost the taste.

Add the nuts to the dry ingredients along with the melted coconut oil and the apple purée. Mix really well.

Empty the mixture on to the lined baking tray and spread out. Bake on the middle shelf of the oven for about 20 minutes.

After that time, have a look, turn it over and rustle it about a bit, then cook for a further 5–10 minutes – but keep checking it's not overcooking. It should be golden, not black.

Let it cool on the tray then empty into an airtight box and store for up to one month.

SWEET QUINOA BREAKFAST BOWL

Serves 2 | Calories per serving 255 | Protein per serving 11g

This has a rather lovely flavour. It's more filling than standard oat porridge and ticks the protein box too. There's also something almost Christmassy about it. This recipe takes a bit longer in the mornings, so it might be worth making up a batch to last a couple of days.

75g quinoa

1 orange

200ml unsweetened non-dairy milk (I used almond)

1 tbsp chia seeds

½ tbsp desiccated coconut

2 tbsp Greek yoghurt

100g raspberries

2 tsp flaked almonds

Place the quinoa in a small pan with 300ml cold water. Bring to the boil and then simmer for 8–10 minutes.

Meanwhile, grate the zest of the orange and then peel and segment the fruit, catching the juice as you do this. Set aside.

Drain the quinoa then return to the pan along with the milk, orange zest, chia seeds and desiccated coconut. Bring to a simmer and cook gently until all the liquid is absorbed.

Divide between two bowls and top with the yoghurt, orange juice and segments, raspberries and flaked almonds to serve.

BREAKFAST ONE-LINERS

- Baked sweet potato (microwave for speed!) with scrambled egg, tomatoes and mushrooms

- A slice of rye bread (or the Courgette Bread on page 108) spread with half a ripe mashed avocado and topped with two grilled bacon rashers

- Leftover cooked rice* fried in a little olive oil with two rashers of back bacon, chopped, and a couple of eggs scrambled up in it

- A portion of the Easy Peanut Butter and Banana Clusters (see page 208) or the Sweet Potato and Walnut Cake (see page 206) over in the Snacks section. Both of these go well with a bowl of Greek yoghurt

- Almond milk, oats, hemp protein powder, berries and Greek yoghurt whizzed up into a smoothie (maybe add some spinach or kale . . . or is that pushing it?)

- Two tablespoons of oats, 10–15 almonds and some Greek yoghurt with raspberries and a dash of cinnamon. Couldn't be quicker!

- A portion of leftover new potatoes, roughly mashed up and fried in a teaspoon of olive oil with a couple of chopped leftover sausages, tomatoes and parsley, and topped with rocket

*Any rice you have left over after cooking a meal should be whizzed straight into the fridge to cool down quickly and used within 24 hours. Cooked rice can easily be kept in the freezer for up to 3 months.

LIGHT MEALS, SOUPS & SALADS

This section is packed with variety and you'll find yourself doubling up on quantity just so that you can take some to work the next day. Imagine sitting at your desk with some of those Thai Prawn Cakes and a flask of Broccoli, Hazelnut and Kale Soup . . . watching your neighbour wade through a sandwich, crisps and chocolate, and knowing you'll have to wake him up in about three hours' time when the sugar crash has got too much for him. Do I detect a faint whiff of smug?

If you're doing your workout at home before lunch, then you could follow all those horrible squats with a delightful plate of Turkey and Chorizo Hash with New Potatoes (which, incidentally, is gorgeous as an After Workout breakfast too . . . No, really).

HUMMUS and ROCKET WRAP

Serves 1 | Calories 310 | Protein 8.6g

If we're calling a spade a spade, then this is basically a folded omelette with rocket, hummus and sun-dried tomatoes inside. But oh, what a lovely combination it is, either for breakfast or a light lunch. You can also knock this up in no time.

1 tsp coconut oil

2 medium eggs

1 tbsp reduced-fat hummus

3 sun-dried tomatoes in oil, drained and chopped

3–4 basil leaves or any herbs you fancy

large handful of rocket, spinach, watercress, any greens . . . you know the drill. The more the merrier

Heat the coconut oil in a heavy-based frying pan.

Meanwhile, beat the eggs with 2 tablespoons of water.

Pour into the hot pan and cook both sides. Slide on to a warmed plate.

Spread hummus over one side and dot with the chopped sun-dried tomatoes.

Line up a ridge of basil, rocket and any other fresh herbs or greens down the centre of the omelette and then roll up to make a wrap. Ta dah!

Annie's Tip: *You can even assemble this on some baking parchment, and then roll up and tighten into position with foil to make a lunch (or breakfast) on the go. Imagine . . . everyone on the 7.32 to King's Cross will be dead envious.*

ASIAN BEEF SALAD

Serves 4 | Calories per serving 211 | Protein per serving 25.3g

This requires one hour minimum marinating, but if you can squeeze it in before you leave the house in the morning, then the flavours will have really developed. Think fresh, zingy and utterly, utterly delicious, this dish scores big points on the protein scale.

juice of 1 lime

2 tsp fish sauce

2 tsp sesame oil

1 tsp tamari or soy sauce

2cm piece of fresh ginger, peeled and grated

1 garlic clove, crushed

450g rump steak

4 spring onions, trimmed and sliced

4 radishes, thinly sliced

1 cos lettuce, roughly chopped

¼ cucumber, thinly sliced

12 cherry tomatoes, halved

small handful of mint leaves, roughly torn

small handful of basil leaves, roughly torn

2 tbsp salted peanuts, roughly chopped

Place half the lime juice, the fish sauce, sesame oil, tamari or soy, ginger and garlic in a non-metallic shallow bowl and mix together. Add the steak and toss in the marinade. Leave to marinate in the fridge for at least 1 hour (or for the whole day, if possible).

Heat a griddle pan to hot, remove the steak from the marinade and cook for 2–3 minutes on each side (for medium–rare, depending on the thickness of your steak), or until cooked to your liking. Remove from the griddle and leave to rest for 10 minutes.

Meanwhile, toss together the spring onions, radishes, lettuce, cucumber, cherry tomatoes, mint and basil.

Slice the steak into strips and add to the salad.

Serve the salad with the remaining lime juice, any meat juices from the griddle pan and a sprinkling of chopped peanuts.

BLACK BEAN BLAST BURGERS with AVOCADO MASH

Serves 4 | Calories per serving 299 | Protein per serving 14.5g

Just as hearty as regular burgers, these guys are a cinch to make for lunch or dinner. Each juicy mouthful really hits the spot and the avocado topping is the icing on the proverbial cake.

2 x 400g cans
black beans, drained
and rinsed

2 garlic cloves, crushed

1 red onion,
finely chopped

good handful of fresh
coriander, chopped

1 tsp ground coriander

pinch of chilli powder

pinch of ground cumin

juice of 1 lime

4 large field mushrooms

1 ripe avocado

2 tbsp Greek yoghurt

dash of lime juice

salt

½ tsp coconut oil per
burger, for frying

tomato, red onion and
gherkin slices, to serve

Preheat the grill to hot. In a bowl, mash the beans to a coarse paste and set aside.

In a separate bowl, mix the garlic, onion, fresh and ground coriander, chilli, cumin and lime juice. Mix well.

Add this to the bean mixture and mix well (vigorously even!) and then shape into 4 burgers and put in the fridge to chill.

Cook the field mushrooms under the hot grill for 2–3 minutes each side.

In another bowl (how many more bowls?!), mash the avocado with the yoghurt, lime juice and a little salt, ensuring you keep the chunkiness. Set aside.

Heat the coconut oil in a pan and cook the burgers for 4–5 minutes each side until crisp on the outside and cooked through.

Dollop the avocado mash on each of the mushrooms, then scoop each burger out of the pan carefully so they don't break and layer them on top. Finish each one with slices of tomato, red onion and gherkin, and serve.

Annie's Tip: *Of course it goes without saying that you can accompany these with a portion of mouth-watering Sweet Potato Wedges (page 180) to make it an After Workout meal.*

BROCCOLI, HAZELNUT and KALE SOUP

Serves 2 | Calories per serving 320 | Protein per serving 12.3g

All those nuts and greens in the same bowl give this soup incredible properties – so much so I think we should we should call it Antioxidant Broth! It scores very highly on the smug-o-meter. Be sure to use the stalk of the broccoli as well as the florets – just as much flavour and lots of fibre.

1 tbsp olive oil

1 small onion, chopped

50g hazelnuts

200g broccoli, chopped

600ml vegetable stock

50g kale, chopped

200ml non-dairy milk

2 tbsp Greek yoghurt

salt and freshly ground black pepper

Heat the oil in a medium heavy-based pan and cook the onion and hazelnuts for 3–4 minutes, stirring occasionally.

Add the broccoli and stock, bring to a simmer, cover and cook for 12–14 minutes until the broccoli is tender.

Add the kale to the pan, cover and cook for 1–2 minutes.

Remove from the heat, stir in the milk and, using a hand-held blender, blitz until smooth.

Season to taste, then serve with a dollop of Greek yoghurt in the soup.

CREAMY CORONATION CHICKEN SALAD

Serves 2 | Calories per serving 343 | Protein per serving 27.7g

Mention the 'lettuce' word to my daughters and they always think 'diety' food. This dish puts them straight. The combination of chicken and a creamy mayo dressing adorning a plate of greenery gets them every time.

2 skinless chicken breasts

juice of ½ lemon, plus an extra squirt

70g frozen peas

170g Greek yoghurt

2 tsp good-quality mayonnaise (sugar-free)

25g raw cashew nuts

2 spring onions, finely chopped

½ tsp mild curry powder

10 cherry tomatoes, chopped

lots of crisp salad leaves, to serve (or even floppy ones . . . just pile 'em on)

salt and freshly ground black pepper

Preheat the oven to 180°C/160°C Fan/Gas 4. Place each chicken breast on a square of foil and squeeze over the lemon juice, then add a little seasoning. Wrap them up loosely, place on a baking tray and bake in the oven for about 20 minutes. When cooked, open the parcels and leave to cool a little.

Cook the peas according to the packet instructions, drain and set aside.

Meanwhile, in a bowl, mix the yoghurt, mayonnaise, nuts, chopped spring onions, curry powder and tomatoes. Season with black pepper and a squirt of lemon juice.

Chop up the chicken into chunks and add it to the mayo mixture, along with the peas. Pile on to a bed of leaves and serve.

Annie's Tip: *Two tips for the price of one here. If nuts aren't your thing, you can replace them with half a can of drained chickpeas – it will still be an Anytime meal. To turn it into an After Workout feast, simply add a few cooked new potatoes (and lashings of ground black pepper).*

BROCCOLI FALAFEL
with CELERIAC COLESLAW

Serves 4 | Calories per 2 falafel 195 | Protein per 2 falafel 7.7g

*Celeriac, despite being part of the root-veggie family, is actually fairly low-carb,
so hence we have ourselves a lovely Anytime coleslaw! It goes really well with these
falafel but is also a great accompaniment to plain grilled steak or lamb.*

Falafel

75g broccoli florets

400g can chickpeas,
drained and rinsed

1 garlic clove, halved

1 tsp ground cumin

large pinch of
smoked paprika

juice of ½ lemon

1 tbsp olive oil

1 tbsp sesame seeds

salt and freshly ground
black pepper

Coleslaw

100g celeriac

juice of ½ lemon

1 small carrot,
peeled and grated

25g walnuts, toasted

2 tbsp chopped
flatleaf parsley

1½ tbsp Greek yoghurt

½ tsp wholegrain
mustard

Preheat the oven to 200°C/180°C Fan/Gas 6.

First, make the falafel. Blanch the broccoli florets in boiling
water for 3 minutes then drain and refresh under cold running
water for a few seconds. Drain.

Place the broccoli, chickpeas, garlic and spices in a food processor
or blender and blend until broken down – you may need to scrape
down the sides of the blender a couple of times.

Add the lemon juice, olive oil and seasoning, and blend again
until smooth.

Using wet hands, make 8 patty-shaped falafel with the mixture.
Sprinkle them with the sesame seeds.

Place the falafel on a baking sheet lined with baking parchment
and bake in the oven for 25 minutes, turning them after
15 minutes.

Meanwhile, peel the celeriac and cut into matchsticks (put your
headphones on maybe . . .!). Place in a bowl and squeeze over
the lemon juice to prevent the celeriac from turning brown.

Stir in the grated carrot, walnuts, parsley, yoghurt and mustard,
and season to taste.

Serve the falafel with the crunchy coleslaw. And do a little dance.

COD LOIN with LENTIL and CAPER TAPENADE

Serves 2 | Calories per serving 428 | Protein per serving 36.4

This is a really rich-tasting dish, but thankfully it doesn't leave you feeling heavy! Serve with carrots and peas or mountains of leafy greens . . . because you can never have too much veg.

40g dried red lentils

1 garlic clove

50g black olives, stoned

1 tsp capers

2 anchovy fillets

1 tsp lemon juice

1 tbsp extra virgin olive oil, plus 1 teaspoon for frying

2 x 150g cod loins

1 red onion, sliced

2 tbsp flaked almonds

150g spinach leaves

salt and freshly ground black pepper

Preheat the oven to 200°C/180°C Fan/Gas 6.

Place the lentils and garlic in a small pan with 150ml water and bring to a simmer. Cook for 10 minutes until the lentils are soft and the water has been absorbed. Drain.

Place the cooked lentils in a small blender with the olives, capers, anchovies, lemon juice and the tablespoon of olive oil. Blitz until smooth. Season to taste.

Place the cod loins on a baking tray and spoon the lentil tapenade on to the top of each one, spreading over the surface.

Bake in the oven for 10 minutes.

Meanwhile, heat the remaining teaspoon of olive oil in a frying pan and sauté the onion for 2–3 minutes before adding the almonds and spinach. Continue to cook until the spinach has wilted and the almonds have started to turn golden.

Divide the spinach mixture between two warmed plates and top each one with a cod loin to serve.

LEMON and OLIVE CHICKEN TRAYBAKE

Serves 4 | Calories per serving 311 | Protein per serving 27.9g

A sun-drenched terrace somewhere in the south of Sicily was in my head when I first tried this. I only had to look out of the window at the murky grey British sky to bring me back down to earth. Nevertheless, this dish will fill your heart with sunny positivity.

8 chicken thighs, skin on

8 shallots

1 red pepper, deseeded and chopped

1 yellow pepper, deseeded and chopped

50g bacon lardons

1 lemon, cut into wedges

3–4 sprigs of thyme

1 tbsp olive oil

50g black olives, stoned and halved

300ml chicken stock

salt and freshly ground black pepper

steamed green vegetables, to serve

Preheat the oven to 200°C/180°C Fan/Gas 6.

Place the chicken, shallots, peppers, bacon lardons, lemon and thyme sprigs in a large roasting tin. Drizzle with oil, season and bake for 30 minutes.

Stir in the olives, pour over the stock and bake for a further 10–12 minutes until the chicken is cooked through and golden.

Serve with steamed greens or any other veg in your fridge begging to be used.

ANYTIME

THAI PRAWN CAKES

Serves 2 | Calories per serving 205 | Protein per serving 25.8g

It's worth doubling up this recipe because these fishcakes make wonderful protein Anytime snacks to fill those gaps in the day when you realise you can't last until dinner. So tasty, they are another Deadman family favourite.

300g cooked prawns

juice of ½ lime

2cm piece of fresh ginger, peeled and grated

2 spring onions, trimmed and thinly sliced

½ tsp fish sauce

1 medium egg yolk

small handful of coriander leaves

¼ tsp black pepper

1 tbsp olive oil

rocket salad or stir-fried vegetables, to serve

Place the prawns, lime juice, ginger, spring onions, fish sauce, egg yolk, coriander and black pepper in a small blender and blitz until well mixed.

Using your hands, shape into 8 small fishcakes. Chill in the fridge for 30 minutes.

Heat the olive oil in a frying pan and cook the prawn cakes for 2–3 minutes on each side until lightly golden.

Serve with a rocket salad or some stir-fried vegetables.

PESTO COURGETTI
with BAKED CHICKEN

Serves 2 | Calories per serving 549 | Protein per serving 43.7g

This is a good way of having pretend pasta without the carb hit. If you haven't got a spiraliser, either use a julienne peeler or a regular veg peeler and peel off ribbons. The chicken and basil pairing really works. If you're vegetarian and fancy this dish, then simply replace the chicken with some diced tofu sautéed in a little oil, garlic and a teaspoon of balsamic.

2 skinless chicken breasts, about 150g each

1 tsp olive oil

2 large courgettes

salt and freshly ground black pepper

1 tbsp toasted pumpkin seeds, to serve

Pesto

30g basil leaves

2 garlic cloves

2 tbsp rapeseed oil

50g ground almonds

large handful of baby spinach leaves

Preheat the oven to 200°C/180°C Fan/Gas 6.

Rub the chicken breasts with the olive oil and some salt and pepper. Place in a roasting tin and bake in the oven for about 20 minutes.

Meanwhile, put all the pesto ingredients into a blender or food processor and whizz up. Add seasoning to taste.

Ten minutes before the chicken is ready, slice or spiralise the courgettes and place in a frying pan with a tablespoon of water. Keep the lid on and steam them, tossing from time to time. This will take about 2 minutes.

Add the pesto to the courgetti and mix well. Turn off the heat but keep the courgetti warm.

Slice the chicken breasts and serve with the pesto courgetti scattered with pumpkin seeds.

Annie's Tip: A crisp, colourful salad of carrot ribbons and radishes is lovely with this. And a bit of colour is so positive for our mood!

LIGHT MEAL, SOUP & SALAD ONE-LINERS

- Chicken, rocket and avocado salad (oh, go on, add a few walnuts, twist me arm . . . 6 halves, chopped)

- Lettuce wrap: iceberg leaf spread with hummus, a slice or two of turkey, avocado and cucumber, then rolled up like a wrap.

- A slice of frittata left over from breakfast (stolen before anyone else gets it!)

- A plate of cauliflower 'couscous' (see Cauliflower Rice, page 192), mixed with cooked lentils, leftover salad veg, some herbs, cumin and a colourful sprinkling of pistachios

- Bolognese beef sauce over Courgetti (see opposite) or Cauliflower/Broccoli Rice (see page 192)

- Stir-fried vegetables with chicken, prawn or beef strips

- Omelette pizza: 2 eggs and extra egg white as a pizza base covered with tomatoes, mushrooms, rocket, avocado and some chopped bacon

- Two cans of chickpeas, lots of cherry tomatoes, rosemary sprigs, at least 6 garlic cloves, a drizzle of olive oil, slow roasted for an hour, makes a lovely gooey, flavourful dish. Eat as it is or on top of a crunchy salad

- A salad of moist tuna (canned or fresh), half a can of cannellini beans, a spoonful of capers and some chopped red onion on a whopping bed of leaves, tossed with some oil, lemon juice and fresh coriander

BEAN and LENTIL CHILLI

Serves 4　|　Calories per serving 284　|　Protein per serving 13.1g

I guarantee every single member of your family (even the most dedicated carnivore) is going to love this. With all those vegetables it has VOLUME . . . and we just love that. Fibre = filling! Plus, swapping the basmati rice for brown rice would add extra fibre.

1 tbsp olive oil

1 onion, diced

2 sticks celery, diced

1 carrot, peeled and diced

2 tsp chilli powder
(more if wished)

75g red lentils

100g puy lentils, cooked

400g can kidney beans,
drained and rinsed

75g sweetcorn

400g can chopped
tomatoes

400ml vegetable stock

275g basmati rice

2 tbsp chopped
flatleaf parsley

2 tbsp flaked
almonds, toasted

lime wedges, to serve

salt and freshly ground
black pepper

Heat the oil in a pan and sauté the onion, celery and carrot for 4–5 minutes until starting to soften.

Stir in the chilli powder, both types of lentils and the kidney beans, and stir to coat with the chilli powder.

Add the sweetcorn, chopped tomatoes and vegetable stock, and stir well. Bring to a simmer and cook for 15–18 minutes until some of the liquid has been absorbed and the chilli is thick and creamy in texture.

Meanwhile, cook the rice according to the packet instructions.

Stir the chopped parsley into the chilli and season to taste.

Serve the chilli on a bed of basmati rice, sprinkled with toasted flaked almonds and with a lime wedge.

TURKEY and CHORIZO HASH with NEW POTATOES

Serves 4 | Calories per serving 363 | Protein per serving 38.8g

I would bet my life on this becoming a firm family fave in your household, so there are major brownie points to be earned here. Quick, tasty, satisfying, brilliant as a packed lunch the next day, this dish melts in the mouth and doesn't cost the earth.

300g baby new potatoes, halved

½ tbsp olive oil

2 spring onions, trimmed and sliced

½ red pepper, deseeded and chopped

75g chorizo, diced

400g turkey mince

2 tomatoes, chopped

100ml chicken stock

1 tbsp chopped coriander

1 medium egg, poached or fried, per person, to serve

Cook the potatoes in a pan of boiling water for 12–15 minutes until tender.

Meanwhile, heat the oil in a large frying pan and sauté the spring onions and pepper for 3–4 minutes.

Add the chorizo to the frying pan and cook for 2 minutes to loosen the spicy fat, then add the turkey and cook, stirring from time to time, for 10–12 minutes.

Drain the potatoes and add to the pan. Lightly crush the potatoes to break them up then stir in the tomatoes and stock. Bring to a simmer and continue to cook for 5–6 minutes until the stock has reduced.

Just before it has finished cooking, poach or fry one egg per person. Sprinkle the coriander into the hash, then dish up on to plates, topping each portion with an egg.

LEEK and POTATO SOUP

Serves 3 (or 2 very hungry people) | Calories per serving 208 | Protein per serving 5.5g

The potato here turns this into a filling and welcome bowl of goodness. It also means that this dish has your carbohydrate quota, so any accompanying food should be Anytime fodder. A couple of chicken drumsticks on the side maybe . . .

2 tsp olive oil

1 medium onion, chopped

2 large leeks, washed and sliced

½ tsp freshly ground black pepper

2 bay leaves

750ml vegetable stock

1 large potato, peeled and diced

250ml non-dairy milk (I used unsweetened almond milk)

¼ tsp grated nutmeg

Heat the oil and fry the onion over a gentle heat for about 4–5 minutes.

Add the sliced leeks, black pepper and bay leaves, and leave to sweat for about 5 minutes, checking every now and then that the mixture isn't sticking.

Add the stock and diced potato, turn the heat up and bring to the boil. Reduce the heat and leave to simmer for 20 minutes.

Add the milk and nutmeg, and cook for another 3 minutes until warmed through.

Leave to cool slightly then blend until smooth and creamy.

ROASTED ROOTS with LENTILS

Serves 4 | Calories per serving 283 | Protein per serving 8.9g

All the laborious veg chopping here is so worth it. Chop them all – then have a little lie-down. This recipe is for four but it freezes well and can be eaten cold in a salad.

1 aubergine,
cut into chunks

2 courgettes,
cut into chunks

1 red onion,
cut into chunks

1 red pepper, deseeded
and cut into chunks

1 green pepper, deseeded
and cut into chunks

1 parsnip, peeled and cut
into chunks

4 garlic cloves, unpeeled

½ sweet potato (about
175g), peeled and cut
into chunks

2 tbsp olive oil

2 sprigs of rosemary

400g can cooked green
or brown lentils, drained
and rinsed

salt and freshly ground
black pepper

2 tbsp pumpkin seeds
and a little yoghurt,
to serve

Preheat the oven to 180°C/160°C Fan/Gas 4.

Throw all the chopped vegetables and garlic into a heavy-based roasting tin and mix well with the oil.

Chop one sprig of rosemary up quite finely and scatter into the tray. Leave the other one whole as it looks weirdly sophisticated when it's burnt!

Season well and cover with foil. Place in the oven for at least 30 minutes but keep an eye on it.

Take the foil off and add the drained lentils. Stir and cook again for another 15 minutes, leaving the foil off, but again keep popping back to check that it doesn't burn.

Meanwhile, toast the pumpkin seeds carefully in a dry frying pan for 3–4 minutes.

Serve the roasted veg and lentil mixture, topped with a blob of yoghurt with the seeds scattered over.

Annie's Tip: This sounds weird, but a few spoonfuls of this mixed with a little Greek yoghurt makes a fantastic filling for a jacket potato for another day's After Workout meal. Versatile or what?

WARM TUNA and NEW POTATO SALAD with CREAMY TAHINI DRESSING

Serves 2 | Calories per serving 441 | Protein per serving 28.5g

The tahini really raises the nutritional profile of this dish. Sesame seeds are packed with calcium, iron, phosphorus, magnesium, vitamin B1 . . . the list goes on. The fresh tuna (unlike canned) gives us our omega-3 fats, which of course reduce inflammation, thin our blood and aid brain function. (I can always do with a bit of that.)

150g new potatoes, halved

3 tbsp olive oil

1 garlic clove, crushed

1 tsp wholegrain mustard

juice of ½ lime

1 tbsp tahini paste

200g tuna steak

75g sugar snaps, sliced lengthways

loads of Little Gem lettuce leaves, shredded

100g roasted red peppers from a jar, drained and sliced

freshly ground black pepper

Cook the potatoes in a pan of boiling water for 12–15 minutes until tender.

Meanwhile, make the dressing by whisking together 2 tablespoons of the olive oil, the garlic, mustard, lime juice and tahini paste.

Heat the remaining oil in a small frying pan and cook the tuna steak seasoned with black pepper, for 3–4 minutes on each side, so it retains a little pinkness in the middle. Set aside to rest.

Drain the potatoes and refresh under cold running water.

Place the potatoes in a bowl with the sugar snaps, Little Gem and peppers. Slice the tuna into large chunks and add to the bowl.

Pour the dressing over the salad and toss together (with attitude) before serving.

SALMON, LEMON and PEA PENNE

Serves 2 | Calories per serving 531 | Protein per serving 28.2g

Just because we're taking a rest from wheat, doesn't mean we have to dodge pasta. There are so many lovely wheat-free varieties in the shops – this one works well. The lemon and pea thing going on really makes the salmon taste special, and of course the prep time is minimal. If you want to make this as an Anytime meal then you can use Courgetti (see page 134) instead.

175g raw buckwheat pasta penne (makes 350g cooked)

2 tsp olive oil

1 garlic clove, chopped

3 handfuls of peas (no need to defrost if they're frozen)

100g smoked salmon, chopped

1 tbsp snipped chives

grated zest of ½ lemon

100g full-fat Greek yoghurt

salt and freshly ground black pepper

crunchy mixed salad, to serve

Cook the pasta according to the packet instructions and set aside your 350g (any leftovers can be made into a packed-lunch salad). I would test the pasta before you take it off the boil. Some brands require a little more cooking.

Heat the oil in a pan and sauté the chopped garlic slowly for a couple of minutes. Add the peas, cook for a further 2–3 minutes (or longer if the peas are frozen, as the excess moisture will need to be cooked off).

In a bowl, mix the chopped salmon, chives and lemon zest with the yoghurt.

Pour this mixture into the pan with the peas and garlic, then add the cooked pasta. Mix well, warm through if desired and season. Serve with a whopping crunchy mixed salad.

SPICED SWEET POTATO and CASHEW STUFFED MUSHROOMS

Serves 2 | Calories per serving 433 | Protein per serving 12.2g

This combination of sweet potato and cashew nuts with a spicy yoghurt sauce is utterly decadent. You won't be able to hold yourself back.

1½ tbsp olive oil

1 small onion, sliced

375g sweet potato, peeled and chopped into large dice

4 portobello mushrooms

50g raw cashew nuts

25g pumpkin seeds

1½ tbsp Greek yoghurt

1 tsp harissa paste

1 tbsp chopped coriander, plus extra to serve

salt and freshly ground black pepper

steamed green cabbage, to serve

Preheat the oven to 200°C/180°C Fan/Gas 6.

Heat 1 tablespoon of the oil in a frying pan and cook the onion and sweet potato for 6–8 minutes, stirring often, until they start to soften.

Remove the stalks from the mushrooms, finely chop them and add to the frying pan. Cook for 1–2 minutes then add the cashew nuts and pumpkin seeds. Cook for another 3–4 minutes.

Meanwhile, place the mushroom caps in a roasting tin and drizzle with the remaining oil. Bake in the oven for 8 minutes.

Stir the yoghurt and harissa paste into the sweet potato mixture, and cook for 2 minutes. Stir in the chopped coriander and season to taste.

Remove the mushrooms from the oven, spoon in the sweet potato mixture and return to the oven for another 5 minutes.

Serve sprinkled with coriander and with some steamed green cabbage alongside. Delicious!

CHICKEN and CASHEW STIR FRY

Serves 4 | Calories per serving 348 | Protein per serving 31.2g

You know that hopeful trip to the fridge we all make once in a while (read: every day) looking for some nice leftovers to pick at? Well, this dish is perfect for that next-day lunchtime scavenge. It's delicious cold as well as hot. And just look at that protein level!

25g coconut oil

½ tsp cumin seeds

½ tsp coriander seeds

½ tsp mustard seeds

1 red onion, chopped

450g chicken breast, sliced into strips

1 red pepper, deseeded and sliced

1 yellow pepper, deseeded and sliced

1 carrot, peeled and cut into julienne strips

¼ Savoy cabbage, shredded

250g basmati rice

2 tbsp cashew nuts

1 tbsp tamari or soy sauce

Melt the coconut oil in a wok over a medium heat and add the spices. When the mustard seeds start to 'pop' add the onion and chicken, and stir-fry for 4–5 minutes.

Add the remaining vegetables and stir-fry for 8–10 minutes until the vegetables are 'al dente' – just beginning to soften but still with a bit of bite.

Meanwhile, cook the rice according to the packet instructions.

Add the cashew nuts and tamari or soy to the stir fry and cook for another 2–3 minutes.

Drain the rice and serve alongside the stir fry (or if, like me, you prefer to mingle everything up and make a mess, then go ahead and do just that).

LIGHT MEAL, SOUP & SALAD ONE-LINERS

- Jacket potato or sweet potato with salmon flakes mixed with thick yoghurt and a little avocado, topped with chilli

- Prawns, avocado, coriander, rocket and a drizzle of mayo wrapped in a Buckwheat Galette (see page 107). Cor!

- Take one of those plastic sachets of cooked quinoa – mix half of one with cooked chicken and leaves, basil, tomatoes and spring onions – delicious hot or cold

- Any of the Anytime recipes with a jacket potato, or some Sweet Potato Wedges (see page 180)

- Open sandwich: a slice of Courgette Bread (see page 108) topped with the Mackerel and Dill Dip (see page 197), and rocket leaves

- Cod and chips – a fillet of cod, and some oven potato wedges

- Any of the dips in Sides, Dips & Relishes added to chopped, sautéed tofu chunks and piled on to a slice of rye bread along with some baby spinach and rocket

- Leftover cooked buckwheat pasta mixed with spring onions, smoked mackerel, cos lettuce and baby cherry tomatoes

HEARTY MEALS

In this section some of the recipes take a bit more prepping, but once you've got your hands dirty with the Beef and Chorizo Burger Stack, you'll be hooked. The Sausage and Potato Traybake is a firm family favourite and couldn't be simpler. It's a perfect reward for your press-ups (and their homework). Again, the one-liner ideas offer quick-fix solutions for those days when you can't be faffed with a recipe.

PORK STEAKS with CREAMY MUSHROOM SAUCE

Serves 2 | Calories per serving 366 | Protein per serving 40.4g

Quick, nutritious, tasty and high in protein, let's polish our halos! Here I've made the recipe with pork but it's just as lovely with chicken or fish.

1 tbsp olive oil

½ onion, finely chopped

2 garlic cloves, crushed

250g mushrooms, washed and sliced

2 pork steaks (about 150g per person)

1 tbsp chopped flatleaf parsley, plus a bit extra for the garnish

100g full-fat Greek yoghurt

salt and freshly ground black pepper

steamed carrots and asparagus spears, to serve

In a frying pan, heat the oil and then add the chopped onion and garlic, and cook very gently for about 2–3 minutes. Add ground black pepper and a pinch of salt.

Add the sliced mushrooms and turn up the heat just a little. Cook for 4–5 minutes until the mushrooms are tender and lightly browned.

Place the steaks under a preheated grill. They will need about 6–8 minutes each side, depending on their thickness.

If the mushroom mix is cooked before the steaks are finished, then turn off the heat and wait. Just before you serve, stir the parsley and Greek yoghurt into the mix and warm through.

Serve the steaks with the mushroom sauce poured over, a sprinkling of the extra parsley and a heap of steamed carrots and asparagus spears. And feel very, very pleased with yourself.

THAI TOFU CURRY

Serves 4 | Calories per serving 314 | Protein per serving 12.5g

This gorgeous light meal is brimming with flavour and so easy to pull together – especially if you delegate the chopping to someone else! Check that your Thai curry paste is sugar-free or, at the very least, sugar features way down the ingredients list. This, lovely Blast-ers, is a really smashing dish.

½ tbsp coconut oil

1 tbsp mustard seeds

1 garlic clove, crushed

2cm piece of fresh root ginger, peeled and grated

2 tbsp sugar-free Thai curry paste (red or green, depending on your preference)

400g can light coconut milk

300g firm tofu, cut into chunks

1 courgette, cut into chunks

1 red pepper, deseeded and cut into bite-size pieces

1 small aubergine, cut into bite-size pieces

125g mushrooms, halved

125g sugar snap peas or mangetout

100g baby corn, halved

5–6 basil leaves

juice of ½ lime

1 tbsp tamari or soy sauce

Place the oil in a wok or large frying pan over a medium heat.

Add the mustard seeds, garlic and ginger, and stir-fry for 1 minute before adding the Thai paste. Cook for a further minute before pouring in the coconut milk with 100ml water. Bring to a simmer.

Add the tofu chunks, courgette, pepper and aubergine, and cook for 3–4 minutes until the veg starts to soften.

Stir in the mushrooms, sugar snaps and baby corn, and cook for another 2 minutes.

Stir in the basil leaves, lime juice and tamari or soy sauce, and cook for 1 more minute before serving.

BEEF and CHORIZO BURGER STACK

Serves 2 | Calories per serving 412 | Protein per serving 34.8g

Yes, yes, yes . . . the ultimate burger is here, hurrah! Oh so pure and without any processed rubbish, the taste is beefed up (pun intended) with the addition of the diced chorizo. It's gorgeous as it is or with one of the relishes or dips in the Sides, Dips & Relishes section.

250g lean beef mince

50g chorizo, diced

1 tbsp tomato purée

½ tsp chilli flakes

1 tbsp chopped flatleaf parsley

1 beef tomato, thickly sliced (2 slices per stackburger)

1 Little Gem lettuce, leaves separated

½ ripe avocado, peeled and sliced

1 tbsp Greek yoghurt

1 tbsp toasted sunflower seeds

¼ tsp smoked paprika

salt and freshly ground black pepper

Preheat the grill to high. Place the mince, chorizo, tomato purée, chilli flakes and parsley in a bowl. Add salt and pepper, and mix together well. Shape into 2 burgers.

Cook the burgers under the hot grill for 5–6 minutes on each side until cooked through.

After you've turned the burgers over, add the slices of tomato to the grill and cook for 2–3 minutes on each side.

Place a Little Gem lettuce leaf on each plate with two slices of tomato on top. Add the burger and then carefully top with the avocado slices. You may need a skewer to hold it all in place!

Top each one with a dollop of yoghurt and a sprinkling of toasted seeds and smoked paprika.

GILL'S ALMOND-CRUSTED FISH with LIME and CORIANDER

Serves 4 | Calories per serving 481 | Protein per serving 40.8g

My sister Gill first cooked this for me while we were on holiday in the Lake District. You'd think after a hard day's walking that only a robust stew would be the order of the day, but this mouth-watering, zingy recipe hit the spot wonderfully after plodding up a couple of Wainwright hills.

Fish and coating

4 large chunky pieces of skinless white fish, about 200g per person

1 medium egg, beaten

6 tbsp ground almonds

1 tbsp rapeseed oil or 2 tsp coconut oil

Dressing

4 tbsp olive oil

juice and zest of 1 lime

2 heaped tbsp chopped coriander (or snipped chives)

1 garlic clove, finely chopped

2 tsp wholegrain or Dijon mustard

pinch of salt and freshly ground black pepper

Start by making the dressing. Simply add all the dressing ingredients to a screwtop jar and mix together. Stand in a jug of hot water and set aside.

Wipe any excess moisture off each fillet. Then brush each with a little beaten egg. Dab each piece of fish in the ground almonds spread out on a plate.

Heat the oil in a frying pan and, once hot, sauté each fillet for about 3–4 minutes each side, taking care not to overcook them.

Once cooked, place the fillets on a warmed serving dish. Some of the almond coating may have come off in the pan – be sure to scrape these bits out too as they're delicious!

Serve the fish alongside a colourful medley of vegetables with some of the dressing poured over and the rest on the side.

Annie's Tip: *If you're clean out of ground almonds, then this recipe works just as well without any coating and just the dreamy dressing drizzled over.*

SAUSAGE GOULASH
with CAULIFLOWER RICE

Serves 4 | Calories per serving 436 | Protein per serving 35.4g

Just saying the word 'goulash' makes me lick my lips. This is a wondrous and easy dish, and the added bonus of low-carb cauliflower rice means you won't be falling asleep afterwards.

½ tbsp olive oil

8 gluten-free sausages

1 onion, sliced

100g mushrooms, halved

1 tsp smoked paprika

400g can chopped tomatoes

4 tbsp Greek yoghurt

salt and freshly ground black pepper

Cauliflower rice

1 medium cauliflower, cut into florets

½ tsp ground cumin

½ tbsp olive oil

1 tbsp chopped mint

1 tbsp chopped flatleaf parsley

Preheat the oven to 200°C/180°C Fan/Gas 6.

Heat half the oil in a flameproof casserole dish and cook the sausages for 6–8 minutes until browned all over.

Stir in the onion and mushrooms, and cook for another 2–3 minutes.

Sprinkle in the paprika and stir to coat the sausages with the spice.

Pour in the chopped tomatoes with 300ml water and bring to a simmer. Cover and stick in the oven for 20 minutes.

Meanwhile, pulse the cauliflower in a food processor to break down until it resembles grains, a bit like couscous.

Put the cauliflower into a roasting tin and toss with the ground cumin and olive oil. Place in the oven, next to the goulash.

At the same time, remove the lid from the sausage goulash and stir in the yoghurt and seasoning to taste. Continue to cook both the cauliflower and goulash for a further 10–12 minutes.

When it's ready, stir the chopped herbs into the cauliflower rice and serve with the goulash, drooling as you do.

Annie's Tip: *You can also make this lovely pretend rice using broccoli instead of cauliflower (see page 192).*

SALMON TANDOORI
with CUCUMBER RAITA

Serves 4 | Calories per serving 326 | Protein per serving 42.5g

This dish oozes health. The ginger, turmeric and garlic will boost your defences and the omega-3 fats in the salmon will keep you full and your hormones calm. What a happy plate of food this is!

200g Greek yoghurt

½ tsp smoked paprika

½ tsp ground turmeric

½ tsp garam masala

½ green chilli, deseeded and diced

1 garlic clove, crushed

1cm piece of fresh ginger, peeled and grated

1 tbsp chopped coriander

juice of ½ lemon

4 x 150g salmon fillets

¼ cucumber, grated

small handful of mint leaves, chopped

vegetables or tomato and red onion salad, to serve

Preheat the oven to 200°C/180°C Fan/Gas 6.

Pour half the Greek yoghurt into a bowl. Stir in the spices, chilli, garlic, ginger, coriander and lemon juice.

Spread the marinade over the salmon fillets, cover and set aside for 20 minutes.

Meanwhile, mix together the remaining yoghurt, grated cucumber and chopped mint to make the raita.

Place the salmon fillets on a baking tray and bake for 8–10 minutes until the salmon is cooked through.

Serve with cooked vegetables with some bite, such as broccoli and green beans, or a tomato and red onion salad. All with a dollop of the lovely raita.

SPICY LAMB MEATBALLS with MINTED SMASHED PEAS

Serves 4 | Calories per serving 357 | Protein per serving 50g

This is a fantastic way to serve lamb. And if you can protect any leftovers, these are ideal for your packed lunch the following day.

Meatballs

500g lamb mince

2 small onions, very finely chopped

1 tsp ground cinnamon

1 tsp ground allspice

a little grated nutmeg

lots of black pepper

1 tsp salt

2 garlic cloves, crushed

2 tbsp chopped parsley

2 tbsp chopped mint

2 tsp olive oil, for frying

Minted smashed peas

1 tbsp olive oil

1 onion, finely chopped

500g frozen peas

small handful of chopped mint

grated zest of ½ lemon

To serve (optional)

1 tbsp Greek yoghurt per person

1 tsp chilli flakes

Preheat the oven to 180°C/160°C/Fan/Gas 4, then make a start on the meatballs.

In a bowl, mix all the meatball ingredients together – apart from the oil – with your hands. Divide into small meatballs, an even number so there's no fighting. About 16 should do it.

Heat the oil in a heavy-based frying pan. Wait till really hot, then seal the meatballs on all sides.

Transfer them (shaking off any fat) to a non-stick baking tray and bake in the oven for 15–20 minutes.

While the meatballs are cooking, make the mashed peas. Heat the oil in a clean pan and fry the onion gently for about 4–5 minutes. Add the peas and cook until any liquid has been reduced, and the peas are mushy-ish. Add the mint and lemon zest, and cook for another couple of minutes.

Take off the heat and smash the pea mixture with a potato masher. You'll enjoy that bit!

Serve the meatballs with the pea mash and, if liked, a dollop of Greek yoghurt and the chilli flakes.

TURKEY BURGERS with PEANUT DIP

Serves 4 | Calories per serving 285 | Protein per serving 24.5g

The ever-so-slightly spicy peanut-y dip really brings the most out of these burgers. Turkey is high in protein as well as L-tryptophan. So what? I hear you say. It's an amino acid that helps our bodies make serotonin, also known as the happy hormone. Time for another little dance, I think . . .

1 tbsp coconut oil

1 red onion, finely diced

1 tbsp grated fresh root ginger

2 garlic cloves, chopped

500g turkey mince

grated zest of ½ lemon

1 tbsp chopped coriander

salt and freshly ground black pepper

Dip

2 tbsp crunchy peanut butter (the no-sugar and no-palm-oil variety!)

1 tbsp soy sauce (or wheat-free tamari)

2 tbsp Greek yoghurt

Heat half the coconut oil and fry the onion, ginger and garlic for 2–3 minutes until softened.

Place the turkey mince in a bowl and add the onion mixture. Mix well with your hands. Add the lemon zest, coriander and seasoning.

Using wet hands, shape the mixture into 4 burgers. Chill in the fridge while you make the dip.

Heat the peanut butter and the soy sauce or tamari very gently in a pan with 2 tablespoons water. Take off the heat and combine with the yoghurt.

Heat the remaining oil in a clean frying pan and cook the burgers for 4–5 minutes on each side until golden and cooked through.

Serve the burgers with the dip on the side and with a large crisp salad or a pile of your favourite greens.

Annie's Tip: *To take care of those risky jar and spoon moments, transfer portions of peanut butter into an ice-cube tray, then simply defrost when you need them. #nodiscipline. Sad but true.*

TURMERIC CHICKEN with SPICED CABBAGE and LEEKS

Serves 2 | Calories per serving 406 | Protein per serving 40.4g

Oh, don't we love turmeric! It not only adds flavour and colour but is a powerful antioxidant too. Curcumin is turmeric's magic ingredient and it's brought to life beautifully by black pepper.

2 tbsp Greek yoghurt

1 tsp ground turmeric

½ tsp freshly ground black pepper

juice of ½ lemon

2 x 150g chicken breasts

½ Savoy cabbage, shredded

1 tbsp coconut oil or olive oil

½ tsp mustard seeds

½ tsp cumin seeds

pinch of chilli flakes

1 leek, trimmed and sliced

1 tbsp desiccated coconut

1 tbsp toasted hazelnuts, to serve

Place the yoghurt, turmeric, pepper and lemon juice in a bowl and mix well. Add the chicken breasts, turning them over in the marinade, then set aside.

Steam the cabbage or blanch in boiling water for 2 minutes, just to soften.

Heat a griddle and cook the chicken (along with its yoghurt marinade) for 3–4 minutes on each side until cooked through.

Meanwhile, heat the oil in a large frying pan or wok and fry the spices until the mustard seeds begin to 'pop'. Add the leek and fry for 2–3 minutes until starting to soften, then add the drained cabbage and desiccated coconut, and continue to fry, stirring often, for 4–5 minutes.

Serve the chicken, sliced, on a bed of spiced cabbage sprinkled with toasted hazelnuts.

Annie's Tip: *Turmeric has advantages way beyond the imagination. It's thought to be of benefit for joints (I personally can vouch for that) as well as serious inflammatory conditions and cancers.*

GARLIC TOFU with NUTTY GREENS

Serves 4 | Calories per serving 329 | Protein per serving 14.5g

This lovely warm salad is a real winner. A whopping dose of good fats comes in the shape of anchovies (vegans and vegetarians can omit these) as well as the chopped nuts. Delicious flavours, piles of greens and essential fats. What more could we ask for?

1 tbsp tamari or soy sauce

3 tbsp olive oil

2 garlic cloves, crushed

300g firm tofu, cut into bite-size chunks

125g edamame beans (or baby broad beans)

180g runner beans, trimmed and sliced

150g Tenderstem broccoli, trimmed

1 leek, trimmed and diced

5 salted anchovies, chopped

To serve

2 tbsp flaked almonds

2 tbsp Brazil nuts, chopped

juice of ½ lemon

Mix together the tamari or soy, 1 tablespoon of the olive oil and the garlic in a shallow dish. Add the tofu and toss to coat with the marinade, then leave in the fridge to marinate for about 1 hour.

When it's almost ready, steam the edamame and runner beans and the broccoli for 4–5 minutes until tender, and then set aside.

Heat the remaining olive oil in a frying pan and sauté the diced leek gently for 4–5 minutes, then add the anchovies and cook for another 2–3 minutes. When done, remove from the pan and add to the beans and broccoli.

Using the same frying pan, cook the marinated tofu and any remaining marinade for 3–4 minutes, turning once. Add to the bean, broccoli and leek mixture.

Dry-fry the almonds and Brazil nuts in a hot pan until the flavour starts to develop and they turn golden. This will take about 3–4 minutes but do keep an eye on them to avoid burning.

Sprinkle the nuts and lemon juice over the tofu and greens, and serve. With your halo gleaming.

HEARTY MEAL ONE-LINERS

- Cabbage leaf tacos! Minced beef cooked with plenty of spice, stuffed into a cabbage or lettuce leaf with a little avo and some Greek yoghurt

- Tofu chunks lightly fried in chilli and ginger, and served with stir-fry vegetables and broccoli or Cauliflower Rice (see page 192)

- A roast dinner! . . . But without the potatoes, parsnips or Yorkshire pud, and the gaps filled with carrots, peas, broccoli and spring greens

- Courgettes, peppers or aubergines stuffed with minced lamb and Lebanese spices (ras el hanout powder is widely available and works wonders with lamb)

- Beef (or turkey) mince dry-fried (or sizzled!) with onion and spices, and topped with yoghurt and some fresh herbs, and served on a bed of green vegetables

- Your favourite portion of lamb, pork, fish or vegan tempeh roasted or grilled to perfection and served with a side of guacamole or one of the dips or relishes in the Sides, Dips & Relishes section

- Courgetti (see page 134) with flaked haddock, a handful of prawns, two chopped hard-boiled eggs, some flatleaf parsley and a lovely sauce made from Greek yoghurt (warmed through) and a teaspoon of olive oil

CHICKEN and TARRAGON CRUMBLE

Serves 4 | Calories per serving 547 | Protein per serving 43g

This is an ingenious new take on the more traditional pie, and miles easier than messing with pastry. The buckwheat, oat and nut topping tastes gorgeous and is, of course, very filling.

1 tbsp olive oil

4 x 150g chicken breasts, cut into bite-size pieces

1 leek, trimmed and sliced

200g mushrooms, chopped

2 sprigs of tarragon, leaves removed and chopped

50g buckwheat flour

200ml chicken stock

1 tbsp Greek yoghurt

25g pecan nuts

25g sunflower seeds

75g rolled oats

60g coconut oil, melted

25g flaked almonds

salt and freshly ground black pepper

Preheat the oven to 200°C/180°C Fan/Gas 6.

Heat the olive oil in a frying pan and cook the chicken for 5–6 minutes until browned all over. Remove from the pan with a slotted spoon.

Add the leek and mushrooms to the pan and cook for 4–5 minutes. Add the tarragon and return the chicken to the pan.

Sprinkle 2 teaspoons of the buckwheat flour into the pan and cook, stirring, for 1–2 minutes. Add the chicken stock and yoghurt, and bring to a simmer, stirring and cooking, until you have a creamy sauce. Season to taste.

Spoon the mixture into a shallow ovenproof dish.

To make the crumble, place the remaining buckwheat flour, pecan nuts, sunflower seeds, oats and coconut oil in a food processor and process until it resembles coarse breadcrumbs, then stir in the flaked almonds along with ½ teaspoon freshly ground black pepper.

Spoon the crumble over the chicken and bake for 20 minutes until the crumble is golden.

Annie's Tip: This crumble recipe also works well as a topping for other meats or a lentil and vegetable mixture. Swap the tarragon for oregano, coriander or any other of your favourite herbs.

ANNIE'S CHICKEN and CHORIZO STEW

Serves 4 | Calories per serving (slow cooker method) 397 Calories per serving with the extra oil (hob method) 419 | Protein per serving 42.6g

A firm favourite of Blast-ers the world over, this is where the slow cooker really comes into its own (see Tip). If you haven't got one, it really doesn't matter – it's still one of those dishes where you can chuck everything together and forget about it. You can also leave out the sweet potato if you want to make this an Anytime recipe.

1 large onion, chopped

2 tsp olive oil

1 heaped tsp smoked paprika

1 tsp fresh thyme

1 tsp fresh rosemary

4 good-sized chicken leg joints or 8 thighs (skin off)

400g can chopped tomatoes

1 heaped tsp vegetable or chicken stock powder

2 tbsp tomato purée

1 celery stick, chopped

2 carrots, chopped

400g sweet potato, cut into chunks

2 bay leaves (it's not a disaster if you haven't got any)

100g diced chorizo

Fry the onion in a large saucepan or flameproof casserole dish in the oil for 2–3 minutes.

Add the paprika, thyme and rosemary, and fry for a further 2–3 minutes. Add the chicken pieces and cook until lightly browned all over.

Add the rest of the ingredients. Bring to the boil and allow to bubble for about 3 minutes, then cover with a lid, turn the heat down and simmer for 20 minutes.

Take off the lid and allow to simmer for another 20 minutes to create a gorgeous rich stew.

Serve with lots of green vegetables to mop up all that lovely sauce.

Annie's Tip: *Put the whole lot in a slow cooker (don't bother to pre-fry the chicken). Turn to high for an hour and then turn down to medium. You can leave it on low all day but, for the last hour or so, leave the lid off so the juice condenses. The sweet potato will have mashed down to create a lovely thick sauce.*

LAMB BIRYANI

Serves 4 | Calories per serving 407 | Protein per serving 31.8g

Yes, I know the ingredients list looks a bit daunting (never mind the overnight marinating), but this makes such a special dish. Ideal for the family or even for entertaining, you will be hoping there's some left – leftover curry must be one of life's greatest pleasures.

200g Greek yoghurt

1 green chilli, deseeded and sliced

3 garlic cloves, crushed

4cm piece of fresh root ginger, peeled and grated

¼ tsp ground cinnamon

¼ tsp ground cloves

2 tsp ground cumin

2 tsp ground coriander

500g lamb leg steaks, cut into bite-size pieces

225g basmati rice

75ml almond milk

2–3 strands saffron

2 tbsp olive oil

2 onions, sliced

1 cinnamon stick

10 cardamom pods, lightly bruised

In a non-metallic bowl, mix together the yoghurt, chilli, garlic, ginger, cinnamon and cloves and half the cumin and coriander. Mix together with the lamb and leave to marinate in the fridge for at least 4 hours, or overnight.

Preheat the oven to 160°C/140°C Fan/Gas 3.

Rinse the rice, then leave to soak in cold water for 30 minutes.

Place the milk in a small pan with the saffron and heat gently to release the flavour. Remove from the heat.

Heat half the olive oil in a wide pan and fry the onions for about 10–12 minutes. Stir in the remaining cumin and coriander, and fry for a further minute. Set aside.

Place the cinnamon stick and cardamom pods in a pan half-filled with water and bring to the boil. Add the drained rice and return to the boil. Cook for 2 minutes then drain and mix with the onions.

Heat the remaining olive oil in a flameproof deep casserole dish with a lid. Spoon a little of the rice mixture in a thin layer at the bottom, then top with half the lamb and marinade.

Top with half the remaining rice, drizzle with half the saffron milk then add the remaining lamb and marinade. Spread the remaining rice on top and drizzle over the remaining milk.

Cover tightly with foil and then the lid. Transfer to the oven and cook for 30–35 minutes until the lamb is cooked through.

COTTAGE PIE with POTATO and PARSNIP ROSTI TOPPING

Serves 4 | Calories per serving 401 | Protein per serving 28.5g

The crunchy rosti topping gives this old favourite a bit more bite. The herbs are vital – even chopped dried ones will do. Serve with mounds of green vegetables.

Cottage beef filling

2 tsp olive or rapeseed oil

1 onion, chopped

500g beef mince (5% fat, if you can get it)

2 celery sticks, diced

2 large carrots (about 450g), chopped into small chunks

1 tsp dried oregano

½ tsp chopped fresh rosemary

500ml beef stock

Topping

400g parsnips

1 large potato (about 220g)

1 tbsp olive oil

salt and freshly ground black pepper

Preheat the oven to 200°C/180°C Fan/Gas 6.

To make the filling, heat the oil in a heavy-based pan and add the chopped onion. Leave to sauté over a gentle heat for about 4 minutes without burning. Turn up the heat a little and add the beef mince, smashing it with a fork into the pan.

After another 5 minutes, add the celery, carrot and the herbs, followed by the stock.

Leave to simmer with the lid off for about 30 minutes.

Meanwhile, you can get on with the rosti. Peel the parsnips and potato, and boil or steam until part cooked, about 15 minutes.

When cool enough to handle, coarsely grate them into a bowl and add salt and pepper.

When the meat mix is almost reduced (just a little juice left over), pile it into an oven dish. Arrange the grated rosti mixture on top.

Brush with the olive oil and cook in the oven for about 25 minutes. If the top singes a little in places, then all the better!

MEDITERRANEAN FISH BAKE

Serves 2 | Calories per serving 369 | Protein per serving 31.7g

Oh goody. Here we are on our sun-drenched Sicilian terrace again – this time for a lovely sunny fish dish. I do love a one-pan meal, it makes life so much easier! It's also worth noting that if you can't face peeling the butternut (despite your newly toned muscles), then use the pre-prepped bags of frozen or fresh squash instead. Failing that, this dish can also be made using halved new potatoes.

350g butternut squash, peeled and cut into bite-size pieces

1 red pepper, deseeded and sliced into wedges

1 red onion, cut into wedges

1 fennel bulb, trimmed and cut into wedges

1 tbsp olive oil

2 x 150g haddock steaks

100g vine cherry tomatoes

few sprigs of thyme

salt and freshly ground black pepper

1 tbsp pine nuts, to serve

Preheat the oven to 200°C/180°C Fan/Gas 6.

Place the butternut, red pepper, onion and fennel in a roasting tin and sprinkle with olive oil and seasoning. Roast for 30 minutes.

Toss the vegetables a little, then add the haddock and cherry tomatoes, and tuck in the sprigs of thyme. Roast for a further 10–12 minutes until the fish is cooked through.

Meanwhile, toast the pine nuts in a dry frying pan until golden and sprinkle over the fish and vegetables to serve.

ROAST CAULIFLOWER, POTATO and BUTTER BEAN SALAD with CREAMY TAHINI DRESSING

Serves 4 | Calories per serving 258 | Protein per serving 7.8g

This might be a little beige in colour but it's certainly not beige in flavour. The spices and the lemon give it a real good kick. Serve with acres of colourful salad.

250g new potatoes, halved

375g whole cauliflower, sliced into strips, core removed

1 tsp ground turmeric

½ tsp cumin seeds

3 tbsp olive oil

1 garlic clove, crushed

1 tsp wholegrain mustard

juice of 1 lemon

1 tbsp tahini paste

400g can butter beans, drained and rinsed

½ red onion, thinly sliced

12 cherry tomatoes, halved

40g watercress

salt and freshly ground black pepper

Preheat the oven to 200°C/180°C Fan/Gas 6.

Place the potatoes and cauliflower in a roasting tin and sprinkle with the spices, seasoning and 1 tablespoon of the olive oil. Gently toss the vegetables together to coat with the spices. Roast for 35 minutes, tossing gently again halfway through cooking time.

Meanwhile, make the dressing by whisking together the remaining olive oil, the garlic, mustard, lemon juice and tahini.

Place the roasted vegetables in a large salad bowl with the butter beans, onion, cherry tomatoes and watercress. Pour over the dressing and gently toss together before serving.

SAUSAGE and POTATO TRAYBAKE

Serves 4 | Calories per serving 527 | Protein per serving 30.9g

I feel guilty that I haven't slaved more over this one, but, frankly, if it ain't broke, don't fix it, as the saying goes. Does what it says on the tin: soothes, comforts, satiates.

8 meaty sausages (gluten- and sugar-free)

2 red onions, cut into quarters

1 small aubergine, trimmed and cut into bite-size pieces

400g potatoes, peeled and cut into slices

about 12 mini tomatoes on the vine

4 garlic cloves

4 sprigs of rosemary

4 sprigs of thyme

2 tbsp olive oil

1 tbsp balsamic vinegar

salt and freshly ground black pepper

steamed green vegetables or crisp green salad, to serve

Preheat the oven to 190°C/170°C Fan/Gas 5.

Place the sausages, onions, aubergine, potatoes and tomatoes in a large roasting tin.

Add the garlic, rosemary and thyme, and sprinkle with olive oil and balsamic vinegar. Season well and toss together, making sure the sausages stay on top. Roast for 30 minutes.

Remove from the oven and gently toss everything, turning the sausages over. Bake for another 15–20 minutes, or until the sausages are cooked to your liking.

Serve with steamed green vegetables or a crisp green salad.

SPICED GREEN BEAN and BUTTERNUT STEW

Serves 4 | Calories per serving 228 | Protein per serving 5.7g

Despite this being more of a hearty end-of-the-day sort of dish, any leftovers will look at you from inside your fridge the following morning in a very tempting fashion. It makes a very delicious After Workout breakfast too!

1 tbsp olive oil

1 onion, chopped

¼ tsp chilli powder

½ tsp smoked paprika

1 tsp ground cumin

2 parsnips, peeled and chopped

300g butternut squash, peeled and chopped

200g green beans, trimmed and halved

400g can chopped tomatoes

salt and freshly ground black pepper

To serve

2 tsp harissa paste

2 tbsp Greek yoghurt

1 tbsp flaked almonds, toasted

1 tbsp pecan nuts, toasted and chopped

2 tbsp chopped flatleaf parsley

Heat the olive oil in a large heavy-based pan and sauté the onion for 3–4 minutes.

Stir in the spices and cook for another minute before adding all the fresh vegetables.

Pour in the chopped tomatoes with 300ml water, season and stir, then bring to a simmer. Cover and cook for 25–30 minutes until the vegetables are tender.

Meanwhile, stir the harissa paste into the yoghurt.

Divide the stew among four warmed bowls and top with the harissa yoghurt and a sprinkling of nuts and parsley.

PEPPERED FILLET STEAK with TURMERIC SWEET POTATO WEDGES

Serves 2 | Calories per serving 509 | Protein per serving 35g

Steak and chips is always a firm favourite and here, with our Blast take on things, we're getting extra nutrients, too. Sweet potatoes, as well as providing your welcome dose of carbohydrate, are also packed with vitamins A and C. And baking them in the oven keeps the crispiness up and the fat content down.

1 large sweet potato, about 350g (unpeeled), scrubbed and cut into wedges

6 tsp olive oil

½ tsp ground turmeric

2 tbsp thick Greek yoghurt

1 tsp wholegrain mustard

2 tsp lemon juice

2 x 150g fillet steaks

1 tsp cracked black pepper

30g watercress

Preheat the oven to 200°C/180°C Fan/Gas 6.

Place the potato wedges in a roasting tin and sprinkle over 2 teaspoons of the olive oil along with the turmeric. Toss well to ensure an even coating. Roast for 20–25 minutes until golden.

Meanwhile, make a dressing by whisking together 2 teaspoons of the olive oil, the yoghurt, mustard and lemon juice.

Rub the steaks with the remaining olive oil then press in the black pepper. Heat a griddle pan until hot and cook the steaks for 2½ –4½ minutes on each side, according to your liking. Leave to rest for 3–4 minutes.

Serve the steaks with the potato wedges and some of the watercress and yoghurt dressing on the side.

HEARTY MEAL ONE-LINERS

- Leftover rice fried up into a lovely mess with diced chicken, bacon, mushrooms and wilted spinach

- An equally delicious mess might be diced tofu, cooked with some black beans, tomatoes, garlic, onions and herbs, along with diced jalapeños, green peppers and some baby new potatoes. Add a tablespoon of nutritional yeast seasoning for extra taste if you have any (see page 25)

- A leftover Buckwheat Galette (see page 107) filled with dry-fried chilli beef and topped with avocado and some homemade no-sugar tomato salsa

- A couple of the Sweet Potato Rosti (see page 101) with a portion of Bean and Lentil Chilli (see page 136) or a couple of scrambled eggs

- A plate of warm protein-rich quinoa, onion, garlic, herbs and chopped vegetables (whatever you have in the fridge or store cupboard), sprinkled with toasted almonds

- A large jacket potato with a portion of beef Bolognese on top (and some chilli . . . oh, and some yoghurt)

- Bacon, egg, sausage, mushrooms, wilted spinach and some new potatoes. Who says you can't have a fry-up?

SIDES, DIPS & RELISHES

I bang on about vegetables quite a bit in this book, so it's only fair that I offer you something more inventive than just a plate of broccoli to accompany your meals. They're all Anytime recipes, as are the dips and relishes, which you can use to cheer up any plate of food. They're also perfect as a side to sizzle up any cut of meat or fish.

PEA, LEEK and KALE MESS

Serves 4 | Calories per serving 105 | Protein per serving 3.8g

The sweetness of the peas takes the edge off the kale-ness of the kale, if you get my drift. This gorgeous mixture goes with absolutely everything.

1 tbsp olive oil

2 leeks, trimmed and thinly sliced

200g frozen peas, defrosted

60g kale, chopped

large handful of mint leaves, roughly chopped

large handful of flatleaf parsley, roughly chopped

large handful of chives, roughly snipped

Heat the oil in a wok and fry the leeks for 5–6 minutes until soft.

Add the peas, fry for 2 minutes, then squash a few of them with a spatula.

Add the kale and stir-fry for 3–4 minutes until the kale softens.

Toss in the chopped herbs, fry for 1 more minute and serve.

Annie's Tip: *You could also stir in 2 tablespoons of warmed Greek yoghurt at the end to give it an extra richness. This works particularly well if your accompanying meat, fish or tofu is sauce-less, so to speak.*

CARROT and CELERIAC MASH

Serves 4 | Calories per serving 159 | Protein per serving 3.6g

This is a lovely simple side dish that adds colour to your plate. I would say it goes best with a heartier cut of meat or a vegetarian equivalent, rather than letting it get lost among the juice of a stewed dish!

750g carrots, peeled and diced

500g celeriac, peeled and diced

2 tbsp chopped flatleaf parsley

1 tbsp olive oil

salt and freshly ground black pepper

Cook the vegetables in boiling water until they are just soft.

Take off the heat, drain and then mash roughly, seasoning as you go.

Stir in the chopped parsley and oil, and dish up!

PEPPERONATA

Serves 4 | Calories per serving 107 | Protein per serving 1.7g

I don't know about you, but I sometimes used to find peppers lurked for far too long in my fridge because I didn't know what to do with them. Now I do! This is lovely on its own (cold, even!) but is also a good side dish to roasted chicken joints, omelettes and the Black Bean Blast Burgers on page 123.

2 tbsp olive oil

1 onion, sliced

1 garlic clove, thinly sliced

pinch of saffron threads

1 tsp balsamic vinegar

2 red peppers, deseeded and thickly sliced

2 yellow peppers, deseeded and thickly sliced

6 plum tomatoes, roughly chopped

1 tbsp torn basil leaves, to serve

Heat the oil in a large frying pan and sauté the onion over a medium heat for 3–4 minutes until starting to soften.

Add the garlic and saffron, and cook for 1 minute.

Add the balsamic vinegar and sliced peppers to the pan and stir to coat with the spices. Cook for 4–5 minutes.

Add the chopped tomatoes and mix well. Cover and cook over a gentle heat for 50–55 minutes, stirring occasionally, until the peppers are soft.

Serve with torn basil leaves scattered over the top.

GREEN BEANS with TOMATOES and OLIVES

Serves 4 | Calories per serving 82 | Protein per serving 3.2g

Lift green beans from ordinary to outstanding! This goes well with any fish or meat, but works especially well with lamb.

300g green beans, trimmed

1½ tbsp extra virgin olive oil

¼ tsp chilli flakes

2 tomatoes, diced

2 anchovies, chopped

12 green olives, stoned and halved

1 tbsp toasted pumpkin seeds, to serve

Cook the green beans in a saucepan of simmering water for about 4–5 minutes until tender.

Meanwhile, put the olive oil, chilli flakes, tomatoes, anchovies and olives in a frying pan and heat very gently, swirling the pan from time to time to ease out the juice from the tomatoes.

Drain the green beans and add to the tomato sauce, tossing them to coat in the sauce.

Serve sprinkled with the toasted pumpkin seeds.

ROASTED CARROTS – TWO WAYS

*Here are two ways to cheer up the simple carrot. Carrots are high in beta-carotene,
which means a good dose of vitamin A. Wrinkle-free skin, here we come!*

ORIENTAL ROASTED CARROTS

Serves 4 | Calories per serving 107 | Protein per serving 1.7g

750g carrots

1 tbsp olive oil

½ tsp Chinese five-spice
powder

Preheat the oven to 200°C/180°C Fan/Gas 6.

Peel and halve the carrots, then slice into long chunks roughly
the size of your middle finger.

Simmer the carrots in enough water to cover them for about
5 minutes. They shouldn't be cooked through.

Drain and scatter in a roasting tin with the olive oil and the Chinese
five-spice powder. Mix well to coat the carrots in the oil and powder
and roast at the top of the oven for 20–25 minutes. Check them
halfway through and give them a stir to avoid sticking and burning.

CUMIN ROASTED CARROTS

Serves 4 | Calories per serving 107 | Protein per serving 1.7g

750g carrots

1 bay leaf

1 sprig of rosemary

1 tbsp olive oil

2 tsp cumin seeds

Follow steps 1–3 as above, but add the bay leaf and rosemary to
the simmering water.

Drain and tip into the roasting tin with the oil and the cumin
seeds scattered over and mix well. Roast for 20–25 minutes,
again checking halfway through cooking to give them a little turn.

WARM BEETROOT, LEEK and WALNUT SALAD

Serves 4 | Calories per serving 192 | Protein per serving 3.7g

Bit extravagant for a side dish, you might be thinking . . . Yes, but we're worth it, aren't we? Added to a simple cut of grilled meat or fish, this makes a filling, delicious and highly nutritious dish.

1 tbsp olive oil

2 leeks, trimmed and thinly sliced

¼ tsp caraway seeds

¼ tsp chilli flakes

50g walnuts, roughly chopped

200g cooked beetroot, cut into wedges

40g watercress

1 tbsp extra virgin olive oil

1 tsp balsamic vinegar

salt and freshly ground black pepper

Heat the oil in a large frying pan and sauté the leeks with the caraway and chilli for 4–5 minutes until the leeks start to soften.

Add the walnuts and cook for a further minute before adding the beetroot, then cook for 2–3 minutes to warm through.

Remove the pan from the heat and stir in the watercress, to wilt it.

Drizzle over the extra virgin olive oil and the vinegar. Season and serve. If you'd like to bulk it out some more, then simply add more watercress and some crisp salad leaves.

CAULIFLOWER RICE

Serves 4 | Calories per portion 52 | Protein per portion 4g

These pretend carbs do a fantastic job of mimicking rice or couscous or any other starchy grain. You could try mixing broccoli and cauliflower rice too.

1 whole cauliflower (800g–1kg), leaves removed

1 tbsp olive oil

salt and freshly ground black pepper

spices, garlic and lemon juice (optional)

fresh chopped flatleaf parsley (optional)

Preheat the oven to 200°C/180°C Fan/Gas 6 and line a baking tray with baking parchment.

Divide the cauliflower into chunks and either use a food processor, which will give you finer grains, or grate it, which might mean some larger chunks (and possibly part of your fingers, too, so take care!).

Spread out the rice on the lined baking tray, add the oil, some seasoning and any flavourings you like (cumin seeds work well, as does garlic and lemon juice).

Roast for about 12 minutes, giving it a little mix halfway through. Some fresh chopped parsley stirred through at the end makes it totally fabulous.

BROCCOLI RICE

Serves 4 | Calories per portion 68 | Protein per portion 5.6g

Here's something a little more creative than just a portion of peas. If you haven't got a food processor, just use your hand grater or a large knife, which takes more time but is great for the biceps.

2 heads of broccoli (about 400g each), broken into florets

1 tsp coconut oil

salt and freshly ground black pepper

Simply put the broccoli, including the stalks, into a food processor and pulse, about a minute at a time, until it resembles breadcrumbs or rice.

Heat the oil in a frying pan or wok and add the broccoli. Cook lightly for 2–3 minutes until bright green and still has some bite.

Season with salt and pepper and add any herbs or flavourings, if you like, according to the recipe you are using.

CARROT and CARAWAY DIP

Makes 6 portions | Calories per portion 92 | Protein per portion 2.9g

The pungent garlic and caraway flavour goes brilliantly with lamb meatballs or scooped up with celery sticks for an easy snack.

700g carrots

1 tbsp olive oil

2 tsp caraway seeds

4 whole garlic cloves

100g thick Greek yoghurt

Preheat the oven to 190°C/170°C Fan/Gas 5.

Peel the carrots and place in a baking tray with the olive oil, caraway seeds and whole garlic cloves.

Cover the tray with foil and cook for about 45 minutes. Check after about 30 minutes to make sure they aren't burning.

Empty the carrots into a food processor (scraping off the best bits!), add the yoghurt and pulse until a thick, slightly coarse texture is reached. Serve with a flourish.

CREAMY HERB DIP (or DRESSING)

Serves 2 | Calories per serving 85 | Protein per serving 8.5g

If you need a quick and easy way to add something saucy to your plate, then this is it. It goes with just about everything!

170g thick Greek yoghurt

1 tsp Dijon mustard

2 tsp no-sugar full-fat mayonnaise

1 tbsp chopped mixed fresh herbs (parsley, basil, dill)

lashings of black pepper

squirt of lemon juice

Mix all the ingredients together vigorously in a bowl and store in the fridge until you are ready to lavish it on your salad, smoked fish, cut of meat, meatballs, burgers, cherry tomatoes, stuffed mushrooms . . . Shall I go on?

Annie's Tip: *You can omit the herbs and add chopped capers instead if the dip is to be served with fish. It is also good warmed through, so give it a few seconds in the microwave.*

RED LENTIL and CORIANDER RELISH

Serves 4 | Calories per serving 123 | Protein per serving 7g

How something so lovely can come out of those funny little orange pulses I'll never know. This is cheap, easy and nutritious. A saint among dishes.

2 tsp coconut oil

1 small onion, diced

1 garlic clove, chopped

½ tsp ground turmeric

½ tsp ground cumin

½ tsp garam masala

150g dried red lentils

400ml vegetable stock

1 bay leaf

2 tbsp chopped fresh coriander

Melt the coconut oil in a large pan and sauté the onion and garlic for 3–4 minutes. Then add the spices and cook for a further 3 minutes.

Add the lentils and cook for another minute or so, then add the stock and bay leaf.

Bring to a simmer and cook for 20–25 minutes, stirring to prevent sticking. Check the lentils are cooked – it should be a delicious orange pulp. Add a touch more water if you prefer a thinner consistency. Stir in the chopped coriander and serve.

Annie's Tip: *This goes well tucked inside both the Buckwheat Galettes (see page 107) and the Savoury Pancakes (see page 199).*

SPINACH with CARAMELISED ONION and SUMAC

Serves 4 | Calories per serving 115 | Protein per serving 4g

Sumac is widely available in supermarkets and is a versatile spice with a kind of tangy lemony flavour. The sumac bush is native to the Middle East, so this recipe has a Lebanese slant to it. The ruby-like appearance of the pomegranate seeds among the green is rather snazzy.

1 tbsp olive oil

1 large onion, sliced

1 tsp sumac

½ tsp smoked paprika

250g spinach leaves

2 tbsp pistachio nuts, chopped

2 tbsp pomegranate seeds – yes, technically, a fruit, but we're looking on them as a very low-carb garnish

Heat the oil in a large frying pan and fry the onion over a medium heat for 8–10 minutes until it starts to turn golden and sweet.

Sprinkle in the sumac and paprika, stir to coat the onion and cook for a further 1–2 minutes.

Add the spinach in large handfuls at a time, stirring them slowly to wilt down.

Sprinkle in the pistachios and pomegranate seeds, and serve.

Annie's Tip: *You can buy frozen pomegranate seeds in some supermarkets, but if you're going through the painstaking process of removing them from the fresh fruit, first roll the fruit to loosen the seeds. Then cut into two halves and hold each half over a bowl of water and squeeze to release the seeds, helping the process along with your hands. Finally, rinse and drain the seeds, and discard the pith and peel.*

MACKEREL and DILL DIP

Makes 4 (snack-sized) servings | Calories per serving 101 | Protein per serving 7.5g

Embarrassingly easy, this is lovely served in a crisp lettuce boat for an Anytime snack.
It's also good in a baked sweet potato – the sweet and salty flavours work brilliantly.

2 x 120g cans mackerel fillets in brine, drained

2 tbsp chopped fresh dill

100g thick Greek yoghurt

juice of ½ lemon

salt and freshly ground black pepper

½ tsp chilli flakes (optional)

Mash the drained fish in a bowl, so no big lumps remain.

Add all the other ingredients gradually. Have a little taste and decide if it needs the chilli flakes. Store in the fridge until needed.

WATERCRESS and AVOCADO DIP

Serves 2 | Calories per serving 115 | Protein per serving 7.5g

Full of iron and good fats – and of course colour! This is a great accompaniment
to the Beef and Chorizo Burger Stack on page 152 (more iron!) or a grilled lamb
steak. It also makes a nutritious topping for cold cuts of chicken.

1 handful of fresh watercress, washed and roughly torn

1 ripe avocado

1 garlic clove, crushed

100g Greek yoghurt

dash of fresh lime juice

½ small red chilli, finely chopped

salt and freshly ground black pepper

Put all the ingredients into blender or food processor and whizz up until green and creamy. Failing that, chop, dice and smash it all together. It will taste just as nice but will have a slightly coarser texture.

Have a taste to check the seasoning, then pop in the fridge until you need it. Have a bet with yourself to see how long it is before the children say, 'What's that green gunk?'

SNACKS

A few words about eating in between meals, which is essentially what snacking is.

'Uh oh, I can feel a talking-to coming on . . .'

Snacks. The word smacks of mindless eating. Eating out of boredom, disgruntlement or just to while away the time. However, people have busy lives and structured mealtimes aren't always possible, so we need to have some flexibility.

These are food ideas for when the gaps between meals seem too long. The Anytime snacks can be eaten at any time, but only to appease hunger, not boredom, lethargy or because you are worried about your child's French test tomorrow.

The After Workout snacks count as your portion of post-workout carbohydrate for that day, *not* as an extra. You might view them as 'treat' items because some of them have a cake-y feel.

SAVOURY PANCAKES

Makes 6 pancakes | Calories per pancake 91 | Protein per pancake 4.25g

These are just as good on their own (no, seriously, they are . . . fold them into a triangle like a pancake) or you can have them as a change for a light lunch stuffed with salad leaves and chicken. The main ingredient is chickpea, or gram, flour. Chickpeas are full of fibre and fairly high in protein, so they are a really good choice. One or two is ample as an Anytime snack.

2 tsp olive oil, plus 1 tsp or so extra for frying

½ fresh onion, diced, or 2 tbsp frozen

½ fresh red pepper, diced, or 2 tbsp frozen mixed peppers

125g chickpea flour

½ tsp baking powder

¼ tsp salt

½ tsp ground cumin (essential for the flavour!)

150ml water

1 tsp olive oil

In a heavy-based non-stick frying pan, heat the olive oil and cook the onion and peppers for about 4 minutes over a gentle heat.

Meanwhile, mix the flour, baking powder, salt and cumin together with the water in a bowl and whisk well (doesn't need anything electric).

Add the pepper and onion mixture to the runny flour mixture and stir together.

Using the same pan, melt the extra oil. This will do for all the pancakes.

Drop a small ladleful of pancake mix into the pan and tilt the pan so the mixture spreads to make a thin pancake. Cook for about 3 minutes each side.

Continue until all the mixture is used up.

Annie's Tip: *You can add any herbs and spices you like to the pancake mix. When cooked they freeze well for up to two weeks, if separated between layers of baking parchment.*

COURGETTE and PEA FRITTERS

Serves 2 | Calories 148 per serving (3 fritters) | Protein 4.5g per serving (3 fritters)

You might wonder if you could be bothered to make this for a snack. Well, try them and then you'll see the effort is well worth it. I actually chuck a couple in a salad too, to give it a bit of bite. Gorgeous.

1 medium egg, beaten

60g frozen peas, defrosted

1 small (about 80g) courgette, grated

6 mint leaves, finely chopped

1 spring onion, trimmed and thinly sliced

1 tbsp olive oil

salt and freshly ground black pepper

Place the egg, peas, courgette, mint and spring onion in a bowl and mix together well. Season.

Heat the olive oil in a large frying pan and add 6 tablespoons of the mixture to the pan, keeping them separate.

Cook for 3–4 minutes then flip over and cook for 3–4 minutes on the other side until golden.

FISH GOUJONS

Serves 2 | Calories per serving 253 | Protein per serving 28.7g

You'll be the envy of the office if you take these into work. They would work well as a main course too, with a pile of leaves, some dip, tomatoes, carrots . . . all of it, loads of it . . . and more.

1 medium egg, beaten

1 tbsp chickpea flour

2 tbsp ground almonds

2 tbsp sesame seeds

grated zest of 1 lime

250g cod fillet, cut into strips

salt and freshly ground black pepper

Preheat the oven to 200°C/180°C Fan/Gas 6. Line a baking tray with baking parchment.

Place the egg and chickpea flour into separate shallow bowls.

Mix the ground almonds, sesame seeds, lime zest and seasoning in another shallow bowl.

Dip the cod strips first into the chickpea flour, then the egg and finally the almond mix to coat. Place the coated strips on to the baking tray.

Bake for 10–12 minutes until lightly golden and cooked through.

Annie's Tip: *Don't tell me you've never had a fish-finger sandwich! Some of these goujons wrapped in a Buckwheat Galette (see page 107) with some crisp lettuce? What a glorious After Workout meal that would be!*

CURRIED BEAN PATTIES

Makes 8　|　Calories per patty 80　|　Protein per patty 3.9g

This recipe makes eight little gems, but double up and you have a whole supply of snacks for the week. They freeze well too. Vegans should omit the egg and use a chia egg instead (1 tablespoon chia seeds mixed with 3 tablespoons water and left for 15 minutes – magic!).

75g frozen chopped spinach, defrosted

400g can butter beans, drained

1 tbsp ground almonds

1 tsp chickpea flour

1 medium egg

1 tsp curry powder

1 tbsp olive oil or coconut oil

salt and freshly ground black pepper

Squeeze as much moisture as possible out of the spinach and place in a blender.

Add the butter beans, ground almonds, chickpea flour, egg, curry powder and seasoning. Process until nearly smooth.

Using wet hands, shape the mixture into 8 patties.

Heat the oil in a frying pan and cook the patties for 3–4 minutes on each side until lightly golden. Put aside to cool and then freeze and use as desired.

BLAST BEETROOT SMOOTHIE

Serves 1　|　Calories 87　|　Protein 2.1g

Perfectly portable, this is a lovely gap-filler that is viciously red and makes you feel so worthy and pure. Ensure your cap is screwed on properly and don't have an accident in the car . . . like I did. Groan.

1 peeled beetroot, roughly chopped

200ml almond milk

2cm piece root ginger, peeled and chopped

handful of blueberries (fresh or frozen)

Whizz the whole lot up in the blender and slurp.

Annie's Tip: *You can add a large handful of spinach, which hardly affects the taste and gives you another dose of green vegetables. It turns the colour a bit murky but ignore that and think about the saintly halo factor.*

SNACK and GAP-FILLER ONE-LINERS

- A small bowl of Greek yoghurt, raspberries and coconut flakes

- Hard-boiled eggs and cucumber sticks

- A teaspoon of peanut butter (easy!) mixed into Greek yoghurt on celery sticks

- A slice of leftover frittata

- Prosciutto-wrapped asparagus spears

- Two chicken drumsticks

- A smidgen of smoked salmon on a wedge of cucumber with a yoghurt blob and some dill

- Tuna mayo in half an avocado

- Two rusk-free cold sausages

- Egg mayonnaise on rounds of tomato

- Any amount of vegetable sticks (just the job if you're a boredom eater)

- A slice of turkey spread with hummus and wrapped around some red pepper slices

- Just 15 almonds or 8 Brazil nuts (sooo specific) and a bowl of blueberries

- Strips of smoked mackerel (smelly but delicious) with a handful of cherry tomatoes

SWEET POTATO and WALNUT CAKE

Makes 8 portions | Calories per portion 195 | Protein per portion 4.6g

I know what you're thinking. And no, it doesn't taste of potato. This ingredient lends a lovely colour, moistness and, of course, a big hit of vitamins A and C. Not what you normally get from a cake, eh?

300g sweet potato, peeled and cut into chunks

150g oats

½ tsp baking powder

60g walnut pieces

50g desiccated coconut

1 tsp ground cinnamon

pinch of salt

2 medium eggs

2 tbsp coconut oil, melted, plus extra for greasing

3 tbsp non-dairy milk

1 tbsp apple cider vinegar

Preheat the oven to 180°C/160°C Fan/Gas 4 and grease a round shallow cake tin, about 20cm in diameter.

To cook the sweet potato, steam it over a saucepan of water until soft.

Blitz the oats in a blender to make a fine flour, then mix with all the dry ingredients.

In a separate jug, whisk the eggs, coconut oil, milk and vinegar together.

When the sweet potato is cooked, mash and add to the liquid egg mixture.

Mix all the dry and wet ingredients together well, then pile into the cake tin and smooth out the top.

Bake in the oven for about 45 minutes. Pierce with a skewer to check that the inside is cooked, then leave to cool out of the tin on a wire rack. Delicious served with yoghurt and fresh berries.

EASY PEANUT BUTTER and BANANA CLUSTERS

Makes about 8 substantial clusters | Calories per cluster 153 | Protein per cluster 4.3g

These little gems take no time at all to make. Luckily they freeze well, or you'll be in danger of scoffing the lot. Two of them plus some yoghurt and berries make a great After Workout carb portion.

80g crunchy unsweetened peanut butter

2 large ripe bananas, mashed

150g porridge oats

pinch of salt (optional)

Preheat the oven to 200°C/180°C Fan/Gas 6 and grease and line a baking tray.

Warm the peanut butter in the microwave so it becomes a little more runny. Add the mashed bananas and mix well.

Add the porridge oats and mix really well. The mixture will be quite stiff.

Place 8 blobs (or more if you prefer them smaller) on the baking tray and press down gently.

Cook for 15 minutes, then cool completely before eating . . . er, I mean, freezing.

APPLE, CARDAMOM and GINGER MUFFINS

Makes 10 muffins | Calories per muffin 151 | Protein per muffin 6.2g

Sinking your teeth into a couple of these as your carb portion could make a very welcome change. The addition of the apple cider vinegar is there to make them rise . . . beautifully, as it happens! I don't advise using paper muffin cases as (due to the lack of fat) some of the cake gets stuck to the paper cases, so bake them naked, so to speak.

coconut oil, for greasing

200g porridge oats

100g buckwheat flour

1 tsp baking powder

1 tsp ground cardamom

½ tsp ground ginger

½ tsp ground cinnamon

¼ tsp salt

200ml non-dairy milk
(I used almond)

2 large eggs

1 tbsp apple cider vinegar

1 large ripe banana
(about 125g)

1 large apple, grated

Preheat the oven to 190°C/170°C Fan/Gas 5 and grease a muffin tray well with coconut oil.

Put all the oats into a blender and whizz into a fine powder. You might need to jiggle the blender jug around a bit in between whizzes.

Empty the contents into a bowl and mix in the flour, baking powder, spices and salt.

In a jug, whisk the milk and eggs together and then add the vinegar.

Mash the banana and add to the egg mixture, along with the grated apple.

Stir into the flour and oats, mix well and then spoon into the muffin tray. Bake for 18 minutes. Leave to cool, and then hide in the freezer. Very quickly!

Annie's Tip: *For variety, you can also replace the grated apple with 150g blueberries or strawberries and leave out the cardamom.*

SNACK and GAP FILLER ONE-LINERS

*Remember, any one of these choices will be your After Workout carbohydrate portion.
So if you'd rather have something from this list than, say, a portion of rice, to go
with your main meal, then of course do. Some days you might fancy a portion of the
Power Granola as part of your post-workout evening meal . . . Go for it!*

- A bowl of oats (60–80g), raspberries and soya milk (or yoghurt)

- A slice of rye bread or Courgette Bread (see page 108) with berry pulp
  (berries whizzed up in the blender) and a blob of full-fat yoghurt

- Three rice cakes with a dessertspoon of almond or peanut butter and some
  sliced banana

- Two pieces of fruit and 10–15 nuts

- A protein shake made from almond milk, some hemp protein powder, blueberries,
  2–3 tablespoons of oats and half a banana. Goes down like a dream

- A bowl of Power Granola (see page 114) with yoghurt and berries

- Leftover Sweet Potato Wedges (see page 180) with Red Lentil and Coriander
  Relish (see page 194)

3

THE
WORKOUTS

GETTING FIT, FIRM & STRONG . . .
AND MAYBE A BIT SWEATY

Chapter 9

AN UNDERSTANDING OF EXERCISE

Unless you've already caught the exercise bug prior to picking up this book, and realised what it can do for your body in terms of health and fat-burning potential, then you might try and dodge this chapter.

'Oh, I'll just do the food side of things. I find the hot, sweaty business of exercise so unbecoming . . .'

Exercise, whether you enjoy it or not, will make your body burn fat even when you're not moving. But you do need to do the right type of exercise.

These Blast workouts will fire up your body and your mind. They are the cherry on the proverbial Blast cake.

THE RIGHT TYPE OF EXERCISE

This means using your muscles as well as your heart and lungs. The workouts you're going to do will feature a mix of the following, and don't require any equipment. You just use your body weight.

The strength work (also called resistance training) is performed slowly. It does involve taking your muscles out of their comfort zone, challenging them and making them hurt a bit. That way, you are 'overloading' the muscle and it then adapts to become denser, stronger and firmer. The exercises we perform on the 21 Day Blast plan are equipment-free – all you use is your own body weight. You will not start to look like a bodybuilder, but you will become more toned and strong. Those new, toned muscles will tap into your fat stores to keep your muscles in their newly toned state.

The cardio work we do in the Blast workouts is short and sharp, and is also known as high-intensity training (HIT). That may sound intimidating but, in this book, different levels are catered for. To someone new to exercise,

20 seconds of mountain climbers is going to feel very intense, whereas to someone else it might feel like a warm-up. The HIT work gets us sweaty, compounds what we've done in the strength sections, makes us fitter and burns more fat. In short, this is the bit that at first you will hate, then later you will find it ever so slightly addictive.

'I am so amazed to have started exercising again. I had lost all confidence in myself to do it!'
H.B., London (16½ inches)

WHY WILL EXERCISE MAKE SUCH A DIFFERENCE TO MY RESULTS?

I can better explain this by taking examples of two women:

Let's take person A (her name is Amelia) and person B (Belinda). Amelia is a size 12. She's been doing some strength work (squats, lunges, press-ups, that kind of thing). It used to hurt a bit, but she persevered and got on with it and now she quite enjoys it. Amelia has also been doing short blasts (pun intended) of cardio work to complement this. This keeps her fit, challenged and burns energy. She has a higher proportion of muscle than Belinda (not bigger muscles, just what she has is firmer, denser . . . the posh word is 'lean mass').

Amelia eats a lot but doesn't like rubbish food. Actually, that's a fib, she loves it, but she also likes being in shape because that way, she doesn't keep putting on fat. She has a blowout now and then. You know the drill . . . chocolate, Chardonnay and pizza with all the sides.

Now, Belinda is different. She used to be a size 12 but has crept up to a size 16 despite the fact 'she eats nothing' and does 'sooo much exercise'. This exercise involves walking the dog while chatting to her friend, with the occasional spurt of jogging, although most days, that's pushing it. She's pretty weak, has very little muscle tone, lots of squidgy bits (her words, not mine) and frankly feels a bit despondent.

Belinda also has a shocking sweet tooth and falls prey to cake, biscuits and stodge, which means there is plenty of glucose in her blood – and plenty of insulin – hence the reason for her 'squidgy bits'. Belinda doesn't really use her muscles much (that kind of walking is hardly a challenge), so they stay soft and slack. If they're not used, the body thinks they are surplus to requirements and will eat away at them and leave the fat stores alone (because they're a bit harder to metabolise and the body looks for the easiest route).

The upshot of this is: if Belinda challenged her muscles a bit more like Amelia does, then her body would turn to the fat stores for its fuel and leave the muscle alone.

If we use our muscles in exercise they will become dense, firm and strong, and the body realises that it is an important tissue and it won't try to break it down for fuel. Instead it will turn to our fat stores. Yahoo! To preserve that muscle (and keep it firm) we need to feed it plenty of protein. So the exercise, coupled with the Blast eating plan (more protein, adequate fat, less sugar plus carbs at the right time) can only mean success.

'Oh, Deadman, you make it sound so simple.'

But it really IS that simple.

THE BLAST WORKOUTS

You may already be in a workout routine and are quite fit and strong or you may just be dipping your toe in the water.

Either way, we don't want it to take over our lives, so there are just four workouts to do each week of the Blast plan, of roughly 20–30 minutes in length. (I spent twice that time staring at my phone in bed the other night.) Your body is going to come alive, your metabolism will be reignited and your fat (released from its life in those fat cells) is going to be put to good use.

Before the workout charts, there is a list of all the exercises involved, together with clear photos and a short description, so there's absolutely no chance you'll get it wrong. Or miss it out . . . or pretend it's not there.

The workouts in this book are based on (but not identical to) the actual video workouts of the online Blast plan and, since you are working from the pages of a book (rather than having me, all hot, sweaty and panting on a screen in front of you), they have been made more straightforward. This way you can really focus on technique and get the most out of them.

Please do the workouts in the order they are set out in. You may have to occasionally do a couple of the workouts on consecutive days, but for the most part try and leave a day in between. On your rest days, you can either do no exercise at all or go for a power walk to stretch out your muscles.

THE DIFFERENT LEVELS

In each workout, there are two levels: Newbies and Pros. A Newbie might be someone who finds climbing, say, three flights of stairs pretty tough on the legs and lungs. A Pro is already doing some strength and fitness work or runs, swims or cycles regularly. In the workouts the Pros will be doing more than the Newbies and they will also have less rest. I'm not being mean; it just makes their workout more challenging. And remember, we are trying to 'overload' so the body 'adapts'.

The four workouts are divided up as follows and are clearly laid out in a table for each of the three weeks:

Workout 1: Lower Body and Cardio

Workout 2: Upper Body, Core and Cardio

Workout 3: Lower and Upper Body (and no Cardio . . . yay!)

Workout 4: Whole Body including a teensy bit of Cardio

Before each workout, you must WARM UP. There are four warm-ups, according to which workout you are doing. See pages 219–25 for details on each one. You should never, ever skip a warm-up.

Ever.

At the end of your workout you will need to STRETCH and COOL DOWN. This will help your muscles regain their original length and will also help prevent soreness the following day. Be sure to check the relevant cool-down section on pages 226–7 for each workout.

EQUIPMENT

It's important to me that Blast workouts are accessible to anyone, anywhere, so all the workouts are equipment-free. All you need is a timer (your phone might have one) and some water (oh . . . and a towel to mop up the sweat).

Obviously, if you have a pair of dumb-bells at home and they are waving 'Cooo-eeee' at you, then you may use them in the strength work. This is only if you are already used to exercise. But they are not necessary.

ONE LAST THING . . .

Before you head to the main workout section, you should understand what will happen to your body. We spoke in Chapter 6 about not weighing. I'm just going to prod you again about that, by saying this: a pound of nice toned muscle that has been through a few Blast workouts occupies a smaller confined space on your body than a pound of spread-out wobbly fat.

'Tell it how it is, why don't you?'

But as our muscles become more toned and dense (not bigger), they become a little heavier. So although you may weigh more, you will be getting smaller.

Hold that thought . . .

'I never imagined that Blast would be the thing to actually get me through the week, actually give me energy, give me an incredible sense of achievement and feel that I am not neglecting myself as we mums often do. It's been a revelation, I have to say! I am new to regular exercise and I am really enjoying it. So thank you . . . it's helped me manage stress and sleep deprivation and stay sane.'

M.S., London

THE WARM-UPS

It's very tempting to avoid this bit and head straight into the main workout, but your joints need lubricating, and your muscles – not to mention your mental focus – do need warming up! Perform all of the following slowly.

FOR LOWER BODY WORKOUTS

[Repeat this list 3 times]

GLUTE OPENERS 6 REPS

Drop down into a squat position with your toes slightly turned out. Push your knees outwards slowly. This will activate your glutes (these are your bottom muscles . . . they're big, so the stronger they become, the more energy they will use up). Then relax your knees inwards and come up slowly between each rep.

SLOW MOUNTAIN CLIMBERS 6 REPS (3 EACH LEG)

From a press-up position on the floor, drive one knee towards your chest and hold there for a split second. Replace. Repeat with the other leg.

SQUATS 10 REPS

With feet hip-width apart, lower yourself down slowly so your hips are almost level with your knees. Squeeze your glutes to drive yourself back up.

FORWARD ALTERNATING LUNGES 6 REPS (3 EACH LEG)

From a standing position, step forwards with one leg and lower your hips towards the floor, then come back to a standing position. Repeat with the other leg.

STAR JUMPS 10 REPS

Also called jumping jacks. Jump both legs out and in, and let the arms do the same. For a low-impact version: just tap each leg and arm alternately out to the side.

FOR UPPER BODY AND CORE WORKOUTS

[Repeat this page 3 times]

ARM CIRCLES (4 EACH WAY)

Circle your arms (either straight or bent) forwards and back at the shoulder joint.

LOW-IMPACT LADDER CLIMBS
10 REPS (5 EACH SIDE)

Stand with your arms in the air and drive one knee up to your chest, at the same time bringing your elbows down to meet the knee.

INCHWORMS 4 REPS

Stand tall. Roll down to the floor, walk out into a plank position, without your knees touching the floor, if possible. Then lift your hips up and walk your hands back. Stand. Repeat.

SQUATS 10 REPS

With feet hip-width apart, lower yourself down slowly so your hips are almost level with your knees. Squeeze your glutes to drive yourself back up.

FOR LOWER AND UPPER BODY WORKOUTS

[Repeat these pages 3 times]

SQUATS 6 REPS

With feet hip-width apart, lower yourself down slowly so your hips are almost level with your knees. Squeeze your glutes to drive yourself back up.

SLOW MOUNTAIN CLIMBERS
10 REPS (5 EACH LEG)

From a press-up position on the floor, drive one knee towards your chest.

GLUTE OPENERS 6 REPS

Drop down into a squat position with your toes slightly turned out. Push your knees outwards slowly. This will activate your glutes. Then relax your knees inwards and come up between reps.

LOW-IMPACT LADDER CLIMBS
10 REPS (5 EACH SIDE)

Stand with your arms in the air and drive one knee up to your chest, at the same time bringing your elbows down to meet the knee.

EASY PRESS-UPS 4 REPS

Get on to all fours, then slide your knees back a little. Ensure your head is beyond your hands. Lower yourself towards the floor (you don't have to touch it) then push back up as if you were pushing the floor away from you.

FOR WHOLE BODY WORKOUTS

[Repeat this page 3 times]

SQUATS 6 REPS

With feet hip-width apart, lower yourself down slowly so your hips are almost level with your knees. Squeeze your glutes to drive yourself back up.

EASY PRESS-UPS 4 REPS

Get on to all fours, then slide your knees back a little. Ensure your head is beyond your hands. Lower yourself towards the floor (you don't have to touch it) then push back up as if you were pushing the floor away from you.

STAR JUMPS 10 REPS

Also called jumping jacks. Jump both legs out and in, and let the arms follow suite. For a low-impact version: just tap each leg alternately out to the side.

FORWARD ALTERNATING LUNGES 6 REPS (3 EACH LEG)

From a standing position, step forwards with one leg and lower your hips towards the floor, then come back to a standing position.

'The Blast plan has helped me (in the menopause) to get fitter and healthier. I've known for a few years that I should get on top of things. I was fit in the past and now my muscle memory is kicking in slowly. I really enjoy the workouts. I lack time, so doing them at home in my own time and space is excellent. I needed motivation and I certainly got it from this Plan.'

B.Z., Oxford

'On Day 16 I decided to climb back on my road bike for a 45-miler to Box Hill and back. The improvement in my fitness and in my strength has been amazing and for the first time I didn't look pregnant in my Lycra. Thank you, you are a genius.'

M.B., London

'I am delighted! I've lost a whopping 10¼ inches. Can't believe it. This is a brilliant plan. I am not a gym bunny, and found just half an hour a day in the bedroom a much more manageable way to work out.'

T.L., London

'I really, really enjoyed this. It's easy to follow, the workouts are great (and short!) and there's no excuse not to fit them into your day. The results speak for themselves. I lost 15 inches.'

H.S., Somerset

THE COOL-DOWNS

When you have finished each workout, resist the urge to throw yourself on to the sofa shouting, 'Thank God that's over'. You need to let your heart rate come down, so aim for a short walk round the room or, at the very minimum, tap your feet out on the spot for a few minutes. You will also need to do some stretches so your muscles regain their original length. Do some or all of the following, depending on which workout you have done. Hold each for 20 seconds minimum.

LOWER BACK

Lie on the floor and take one bent leg across your body, pushing down gently on the outside of the knee to increase the stretch in the lower back. Repeat with the other leg.

GLUTES

Lie on your back with your knees bent and place one foot on the other knee. Lift up both legs and feel the stretch in one glute. Repeat on the other side.

QUADS (FRONT OF THIGH)

In a standing position, hold one foot into your glute, keeping your knees together. Repeat with the other leg.

HAMSTRINGS (BACK OF THIGH)

Lean forwards over the stretching leg (which should be straight) and make sure your back is flat. Poke your buttocks up to face the ceiling (sounds odd, but it works) and you will feel the hamstrings stretch. Repeat with the other leg.

CHEST AND FRONT OF SHOULDER

Stand adjacent to a wall and extend one hand out level with your shoulder and then turn away from it so you feel a stretch on one half of your chest. Repeat on the other side.

TRICEPS

Put one arm behind your head and reach down your back, pushing the arm gently with your other hand to further the stretch. Repeat with the other arm.

THE EXERCISES – HOW TO DO THEM

OK, everyone, so here's how to do the moves that make up the workouts. The only way to do this is to jump in with both feet. Read the description then check out the technique using the photographs. Alternatively, you can watch me do the moves in the little 'How-To' clips on our YouTube channel. Just search for Annie Deadman. You'll find the clips included with all our workout videos. A treasure trove of loveliness!

Right, onward with the descriptions. They're a bit serious but it's better to err on the side of clarity!

STRENGTH EXERCISES

LOWER BODY

(in alphabetical order)

CURTSEY LUNGES

Stand with your feet shoulder-width apart and take a big step back and across as if doing a curtsey.

Keep your front foot, chest and hips facing forwards and your back knee should drop to the floor. Feel it in your inner thigh and glute.

Repeat with the other leg.

FORWARD LUNGES

Stand with your feet shoulder-width apart and then take a big step forwards, bending both knees as you go.

Keep your front heel on the floor. Get as low to the floor as you can, then push off the front foot (using the heel) to bring you back up.

Repeat with the other leg.

HIP RAISES

Lie on the floor on your back with your legs bent, feet flat on the floor. Dig your heels in so your toes point upwards.

Lift your hips slowly off the floor as high as you can, squeezing the glutes as you go.

Drop them back down but not all the way to the floor. You can make this more challenging by elevating your feet on to a chair or bed, as this will give you more range of motion.

REVERSE LUNGES AND REVERSE PULSE LUNGES

Stand with your feet shoulder-width apart and take a big step backwards with one leg, allowing both knees to bend.

Push your front foot into the ground to bring the back leg back to the starting position. Repeat with the other leg.

Add a little half rep at the bottom of the move for pulse lunges.

SIDE LUNGES

Keeping your back straight, take a step to the side and bend the knee, keeping both feet facing forwards, not turned out. Keep the static leg straight both through the downward movement and when you come back up to a standing position.

Repeat with the other leg.

SQUATS

With feet slightly wider than shoulder-width apart, and toes facing forwards, lower your hips slowly to the floor, keeping your back straight and your chest forwards (as if you are sitting on the toilet).

Squeeze your glutes a little to bring yourself back up.

SQUATS AND SIDE LEG RAISES

This is a wonderful move for the whole lower body. Start with your feet slightly wider than shoulder-width apart and lower yourself into the squat position as above.

As you come out of the squat, lift one leg out to the side so it's off the floor, keeping it straight, and pushing the toe slightly downwards so you are really stretching the leg. That hits the outside of your glute. Lovely!

Return the foot to the floor just before you're about to go into the next squat and then raise the other leg in the same way.

STATIC LUNGES

Stand with your feet hip-width apart. Take a step forwards with your right leg. Keep both legs straight and your back heel off the floor. This is your starting position.

Now, keeping your back straight and your chest forwards, lower yourself slowly downwards by bending both legs. If you're not used to these, don't go too far at first, just enough to feel it in both legs.

To come back up, simply push through the front heel, but keep the back heel off the floor the whole time.

Repeat the prescribed reps for that leg, then swap and repeat on the other leg.

SUMO SQUATS AND HALF-SUMO SQUATS

Stand tall with your feet wider than shoulder-width apart. Turn out your feet.

Keeping your back straight and your knees facing the same direction as your toes, lower yourself to the floor, then squeeze your glutes to bring you all the way back up. You will feel it more in your glutes and your inner thigh.

Half-sumo squats are the same move as above, but once you've gone all the way down, you only come back up halfway, so you never straighten your legs. Ouch.

WALL SQUATS

Start by leaning against a wall with your legs out in front, then slowly lower yourself so your hips are at the same level as your knees. Your heels should be directly under your knees.

Hold that position for the prescribed time; you'll feel like a real lemon and it will hurt. Big time.

To come out of that position, just push through your heels and stand up.

ABDOMINAL CRUNCHES

The description is quite long here, simply because these are so easy to get wrong!

Lie on your back with your knees bent, feet flat on the floor.

Bring your hands behind your head, overlapped, and bring your elbows forwards a little. As you breathe out, lift your head and shoulders (including your shoulder blades) off the floor so you are driving your ribcage towards your thighs, hold the crunch at the other end for a split second.

Then breathe in to lower back down. Your head can touch the floor but don't rest there . . . go straight back up for the next rep. Don't let your stomach dome up, try and suck it downwards.

You make this exercise harder by having your knees in the air at a tabletop position or easier by running your hands up your thighs and keeping your feet on the floor.

OBLIQUE CRUNCHES

Do the same move, but instead aim your opposite shoulder to the opposite knee. Knees are still either on the floor or – harder – at the tabletop position.

STRAIGHT-LEG CRUNCHES

Lie on your back, legs straight up in the air.

On the out breath, reach up with extended arms towards your feet, bringing your shoulder blades off the floor; lower yourself back down but not all the way to the floor. Repeat. If your neck starts to ache, then support your head with one hand.

CRAB TOE TOUCHES

This is a great move for the arms, shoulders and core.

Sit on the floor with your arms behind you and your feet on the floor.

Lift your hips a few inches off the floor, then lift one leg in the air straight and, at the same time, bring your opposite arm (i.e. your right arm if your left leg is off the floor) forwards to touch it. Aim for your ankle!

Repeat on the other side, keeping your hips off the floor.

DEADBUGS

Lie on your back with legs stretched out and your arms above your head.

Keeping all limbs straight, bring one leg up to meet the opposite arm, as well as your head and shoulders, exhaling as you do.

Return to the starting position (i.e. flat out straight) and then repeat on the other side.

You can make this more challenging by keeping both legs dead straight, about 2 inches off the floor throughout. This really hits the lower abdominals more. Return to the floor if this is painful on your lower back.

HEEL TOUCHES

Lie on your back with your knees bent.

Lift your head and shoulders off the floor and bend sideways at the waist to touch left hand to left ankle, then bend the other way to touch right hand to right ankle. Palms should be facing up.

As you are doing each move, think about trying to slide your hand underneath the sole of your foot. That will really hit the spot. Don't return your head and shoulders to the floor until the prescribed time is up.

REGULAR PLANK

Plank is great for the core and upper body. It can be done at different levels.

Lie on your front, resting on your forearms with your elbows directly underneath your shoulders.

First level: Leave your knees on the floor but lift your hips up so they are level with your shoulder blades. This is a half-plank. Hold that position without letting your back sink down.

Next level: Do as above but take one knee off the floor, keeping one leg straight.

Last level: Both knees off the floor! Take care your back doesn't sink down, squeeze your glutes and tighten your legs to help you. You can make this last version even harder by lifting a leg or taking one arm off the floor.

SUPERMAN PLANK

First level: On all fours, take your right leg straight out behind you and extend your left arm in front so it's level with your ear. Hold for a couple of seconds, then repeat on the other side. Try not to move your spine or pelvis too much. Imagine you have something resting on your back that may spill.

To make this harder: Lie on your forearms as if starting the first level half-plank. Then lift each arm and leg out, first the right, then the left, as above. Do your best not to become lop-sided.

Harder still: Start with straight arms and legs (i.e. on your toes!) and lift opposite arm and leg at the same time, but keep your hips down so your stomach muscles are doing all the work. You'll wobble like mad but it's a great exercise.

SPIDERMAN PLANK

First level: Go into a half-plank position on your forearms with your knees on the floor. Slowly bring the left knee towards the left elbow. Replace, then repeat right knee to right elbow, all the time keeping your back still.

To make this harder: Do the same move but in full plank position, with your knees off the floor. You can be on your forearms or have straight arms.

WALKING PLANK

First level: Get into the same position as for a half-plank, on your forearms, with your knees on the floor. In this exercise, the plan is to go from resting on your forearms to using your hands to push you up.

From forearm position, place your right hand where your right elbow is and push up, doing the same with the left arm, just after.

Once up, return to the floor in the same way, reversing the move so you end up on your forearms. Alternate with the other arm.

To make this harder: Do the same exercise with your knees off the floor. Go on, I dare you.

PRESS-UPS

First level: Start on all fours, hands slightly wider than shoulder-width apart and lower your upper body to the floor, keeping your head beyond your hands, not in between. To come back up, exhale and push, literally push, the floor away from you. This will recruit those chest muscles.

Next level: The same move, but knees are further back and your hips forward a little so there is more weight over your upper body. Keep your spine level and tighten your abdominal muscles as you come back up.

Full on 'get you' version: Knees off the floor, lower yourself slowly, breathing in. Then, again, push the floor away from you to come up. Even if you only do a few, and then have to put your knees down, that is terrific!

PRONE LAT PULL-DOWNS

This works your upper back.

Lie on the floor stretched out and face down. Arms are extended forwards with palms flat.

As you breathe out, lift yourself a couple of inches off the floor (you'll feel this towards your lower back muscles, but that's fine) and bring your elbows down towards your hips like a 'W' shape, squeezing your shoulder blades into a 'V' shape.

Breathe in to go back down to the floor with your arms extended again. That was 1 rep.

CARDIO EXERCISES

These exercises will raise your heart rate, so get you fitter and raise your metabolic rate (the rate at which you burn fat), and that metabolic rate will stay revved up for a few hours afterwards too. Yes, even while you're sitting down at your desk! This is the bit you might hate at first because it feels uncomfortable. But persevere. It's really worth it.

WIDE TOE TAPS

Stand with your feet wider than shoulder-width apart.

Bend your knees slightly then tap your feet really fast, like jogging on the spot but only taking your feet about an inch off the ground. I find pulling a face really helps you go faster. We can look like total lemons together!

HIGH KNEES

This is a bit like sprinting on the spot, but bring your knees up towards your chest. You'll need to pump your arms too, just as if you were sprinting! There is only ever one foot on the ground at any one time.

Easier level: Just walk rather than jog this, but aim the knees quite high.

LADDER CLIMBS

Like high knees but with arms too . . . just as if you were shinning fast up a ladder (as you do). Reach the arms high and pump them up and down, just like your knees.

To take it down a notch, just walk the move briskly but still use your arms. (Don't expect your hair to look marvellous after this.)

MOUNTAIN CLIMBERS

Start on the floor with your knees off the floor, and your arms straight, facing down.

Drive one knee towards your chest, then swap to the other leg. Try and keep your hips low and your back straight. As you get better at this, you will be able to go faster and faster.

OBLIQUE CLIMBERS

You start in the same position as for mountain climbers but aim your knee to the opposite elbow so you are getting a bit of a twist.

SQUAT JACKS

Stand tall with your legs apart and slightly bent.

Jump both legs out to the side and then back, in and out (like the bottom half of a star jump (see opposite) but keeping them slightly bent all the time.

For a lower-impact version, tap one leg out to the side at a time.

SQUAT JUMPS

(You'll soon learn to love these in a hating kind of way.)

Stand with your legs wider than shoulder-width apart.

Lower yourself into a squat and then jump up into the air but land in a squat again, very softly without jarring your knees.

Repeat again. Basically, you don't straighten your legs unless you're in the air.

Easier version: Alternate regular squats with the squat jumps.

STAR JUMPS

Jump both legs out to the sides as if for a squat jack (see opposite) and do the same with the arms. Don't pause after each one, just keep going.

POWER STAR JUMPS

To make them harder (oh, go on): do a power star jump. This involves starting with your feet together, doing a mini squat with your arms by your side, then doing a massive jump in mid-air, taking your legs and arms out to the side at the same time in a starfish shape, then you land with feet together and arms by your side, in that mini-squat position.

Go straight into the next rep. Repeat for the prescribed time . . . not without a little swearing.

SWITCHKICKS

This lovely one is a bit like doing the can-can.

Stand tall, and flick one leg out in front of you, immediately followed by the other leg. Exactly that. Keep your arms by your sides and imagine you are doing your rendition of *Riverdance*.

THE WORKOUT CHARTS

WEEK ONE WORKOUT 1
LOWER BODY & CARDIO

	NEWBIES 20–22 minutes	PROS 25–28 minutes
Section 1: LEGS		
SQUATS	8–10 reps	16 reps
	Rest 20 seconds	*Rest 20 seconds*
FORWARD LUNGES, alternating legs	16 reps (8 each leg)	20 reps (10 each leg)
	Rest 30–40 seconds	*Rest 30 seconds*
Do 1 set squats, then 1 set lunges, then repeat as prescribed	Do 3 rounds	Do 3 rounds
Section 2: CARDIO		
STAR JUMPS	20 seconds	30 seconds
	Rest 20 seconds	*Rest 20 seconds*
MOUNTAIN CLIMBERS	20 seconds	30 seconds
	Rest 20 seconds	*Rest 20 seconds*
	Repeat 3 times	Repeat 4 times
Section 3: LEGS & GLUTES		
SUMO SQUATS	8–10 reps	16 reps
	Rest 20 seconds	*Rest 20 seconds*
HIP RAISES	8–10 reps	16 reps
	Rest 30–40 seconds	*Rest 30 seconds*
Do 1 set sumo squats, then 1 set hip raises, then repeat as prescribed	Do 3 rounds	Do 3 rounds
Section 4: CARDIO		
HIGH KNEES	20 seconds	30 seconds
	Rest 20 seconds	*Rest 20 seconds*
WIDE TOE TAPS	20 seconds	30 seconds
	Rest 20 seconds	*Rest 20 seconds*
	Repeat 3 times	Repeat 4 times

WEEK ONE WORKOUT 2
UPPER BODY, CORE & CARDIO

	NEWBIES 20–22 minutes	PROS 24–26 minutes
Section 1: CHEST & BACK		
PRESS-UPS	10 –12 reps	16 reps
	Rest 20 seconds	*Rest 20 seconds*
PRONE LAT PULL-DOWNS	10 –12 reps	16 reps
	Rest 30–40 seconds	*Rest 30 seconds*
Do 1 set of each, then repeat as prescribed	Do 3 rounds	Do 3 rounds
Section 2: CARDIO		
LADDER CLIMBS	20 seconds	30 seconds
	Rest 20 seconds	*Rest 20 seconds*
SQUAT JACKS	20 seconds	30 seconds
	Rest 20 seconds	*Rest 20 seconds*
	Repeat 3 times	Repeat 4 times
Section 3: CORE		
PLANK (or half plank)	20–30 second hold	30-second–1 minute hold
	Rest 15 seconds	*Rest 15 seconds*
ABDOMINAL CRUNCHES	15 reps	20–30 reps
	Rest 20–30 seconds	*Rest 20–30 seconds*
Do 1 set of each, then repeat as prescribed	Do 3 rounds	Do 3 rounds
Section 4: CARDIO		
SQUAT JUMPS	20 seconds	30 seconds
	Rest 20 seconds	*Rest 20 seconds*
OBLIQUE CLIMBERS	20 seconds	30 seconds
	Rest 20 seconds	*Rest 20 seconds*
	Repeat 3 times	Repeat 4 times

WEEK ONE WORKOUT 3
WHOLE BODY (no cardio)

7 exercises	NEWBIES 21 minutes	PROS 28 minutes
PRESS-UPS SQUATS CRAB TOE TOUCHES CURTSEY LUNGES STRAIGHT-LEG CRUNCHES FORWARD LUNGES SIDE LUNGES	Do each exercise for 35 seconds	Do each exercise for 40 seconds
	Rest 25 seconds between each exercise	*Rest 20 seconds between each exercise*
	Repeat 3 times	Repeat 4 times

WEEK ONE WORKOUT 4
WHOLE BODY (with cardio)

9 exercises	NEWBIES 21 minutes	PROS 25 minutes
SUMO SQUATS	14 reps	20 reps
REVERSE LUNGES	14 reps	20 reps
HIGH KNEES	20 seconds	30 seconds
PRESS-UPS	14 reps	18 reps
ABDOMINAL CRUNCHES	20 reps	30 reps
SQUAT JACKS	20 seconds	30 seconds
SUPERMAN PLANK	10 reps	14 reps
DEADBUGS	10 reps	14 reps
STAR JUMPS	20 seconds	30 seconds
	Rest 20 seconds between each exercise	*Rest 20 seconds between each exercise*
	Repeat 3 times	Repeat 3 times

WEEK TWO WORKOUT 1
LOWER BODY & CARDIO

	NEWBIES 22–24 minutes	PROS 26–30 minutes
Section 1: LEGS		
SQUATS	12–14 reps	16–20 reps
	Rest 20 seconds	*Rest 20 seconds*
SIDE LUNGES, alternating legs	16 reps (8 each leg)	20 reps (10 each leg)
	Rest for 30–40 seconds	*Rest for 30 seconds*
Do 1 set of each, then repeat as prescribed	Do 3 rounds	Do 3 rounds
Section 2: CARDIO		
STAR JUMPS	20 seconds	30 seconds
	Rest 20 seconds	*Rest 20 seconds*
HIGH KNEES	20 seconds	30 seconds
	Rest 20 seconds	*Rest 20 seconds*
	Repeat 3 times	Repeat 4 times
Section 3: LEGS & GLUTES		
SUMO SQUATS	12–14 reps	16–20 reps
	Rest 20 seconds	*Rest 20 seconds*
HIP RAISES	12 reps	16–20 reps
	Rest 30–40 seconds	*Rest 30 seconds*
Do 1 set of each, then repeat as prescribed	Do 3 rounds	Do 3 rounds
Section 4: CARDIO		
WIDE TOE TAPS	20 seconds	30 seconds
	Rest 20 seconds	*Rest 20 seconds*
SQUAT JACKS	20 seconds	30 seconds
	Rest 20 seconds	*Rest 20 seconds*
	Repeat 3 times	Repeat 4 times

WEEK TWO WORKOUT 2
UPPER BODY, CORE & CARDIO

	NEWBIES 24 minutes	PROS 28 minutes
Section 1: CHEST & CORE		
PRESS-UPS	12–14 reps	16–20 reps
	Rest 20 seconds	*Rest 20 seconds*
ABDOMINAL CRUNCHES	16 reps	20 reps
	Rest 20 seconds	*Rest 20 seconds*
OBLIQUE CRUNCHES	16 reps	20 reps
	Rest 30–40 seconds	*Rest 30 seconds*
Do 1 set of each, then repeat as prescribed	Do 3 rounds	Do 3 rounds
Section 2: CARDIO		
LADDER CLIMBS	20 seconds	30 seconds
	Rest 20 seconds	*Rest 20 seconds*
SQUAT JUMPS	20 seconds	30 seconds
	Rest 20 seconds	*Rest 20 seconds*
	Repeat 3 times	Repeat 4 times
Section 3: BACK & CORE		
PRONE LAT PULL-DOWNS	12 reps	16 reps
	Rest 20 seconds	*Rest 20 seconds*
DEADBUGS	30 seconds	30–40 seconds
	Rest 20 seconds	*Rest 20 seconds*
SPIDERMAN PLANK	8 reps	12 reps
	Rest 20 seconds	*Rest 20 seconds*
Do 1 set of each, then repeat as prescribed	Do 3 rounds	Do 3 rounds
Section 4: CARDIO		
STAR JUMPS (add in some power ones!)	20 seconds	30 seconds
	Rest 20 seconds	*Rest 20 seconds*
SWITCHKICKS	20 seconds	30 seconds
	Rest 20 seconds	*Rest 20 seconds*
	Repeat 3 times	Repeat 4 times

WEEK TWO WORKOUT 3
WHOLE BODY (no cardio)

7 exercises	NEWBIES 21 minutes	PROS 28 minutes
SQUATS HALF SUMO SQUATS PRESS-UPS WALKING PLANK REVERSE PULSE LUNGES SIDE LUNGES HIP RAISES	Do each exercise for 35 seconds	Do each exercise for 40 seconds
	Rest 25 seconds between each exercise	*Rest 20 seconds between each exercise*
	Repeat 3 times	Repeat 4 times

WEEK TWO WORKOUT 4
WHOLE BODY (with cardio)

9 exercises	NEWBIES 21–23 minutes	PROS 24–26 minutes
FORWARD LUNGES	14 reps	20 reps
SUMO SQUATS	16 reps	20 reps
SQUAT JUMPS	16 reps	20 reps
CRAB TOE TOUCHES	16 reps	20 reps
SPIDERMAN PLANK	12 reps	16 reps
SWITCHKICKS	20 seconds	30 seconds
HEEL TOUCHES	20 reps	30 reps
STRAIGHT-LEG CRUNCHES	20 reps	30 reps
OBLIQUE CLIMBERS	20 seconds	30 seconds
	Rest 20 seconds between each exercise	*Rest 20 seconds between each exercise*
	Repeat 3 times	Repeat 3 times

WEEK THREE WORKOUT 1
LOWER BODY & CARDIO

	NEWBIES 24 minutes	PROS 28 minutes
Section 1		
WALL SQUATS	30–40 second hold	40 second–1 minute hold
	Rest 20 seconds	*Rest 15 seconds*
SQUATS AND SIDE LEG RAISES	16 reps (8 each leg)	20 reps (10 each leg)
	Rest 20 seconds	*Rest 15 seconds*
SLOW SQUAT JUMPS (pause at the bottom part of the jump for about 2 seconds . . . painful!)	12 reps	16–20 reps
	Rest 30 seconds	*Rest 30 seconds*
	Do 3 rounds	Do 3 rounds
Section 2		
HIP RAISES	16–18 reps	20–24 reps
	Rest 20 seconds	*Rest 20 seconds*
WIDE TOE TAPS	25 seconds	35 seconds
	Rest 20 seconds	*Rest 20 seconds*
HALF SUMO SQUATS	14 reps	16–20 reps
	Rest 30 seconds	*Rest 30 seconds*
	Do 3 rounds	Do 3 rounds
Section 3		
STATIC LUNGES LEFT LEG	10–14 reps	16–20 reps
	Rest 20 seconds	*Rest 20 seconds*
STATIC LUNGES RIGHT LEG	10–14 reps	16–20 reps
	Rest 20 seconds	*Rest 20 seconds*
MOUNTAIN CLIMBERS	25 seconds	35 seconds
	Rest 30 seconds	*Rest 30 seconds*
	Do 3 rounds	Do 3 rounds

WEEK THREE WORKOUT 2
UPPER BODY, CORE & CARDIO

	NEWBIES 24–26 minutes	PROS 28 minutes
Section 1		
PRESS-UPS (try a harder level!)	12–14 reps	16–20 reps
	Rest 10–15 seconds	*Minimal rest*
DEADBUGS	12–14 reps	16–20 reps
	Rest 10–15 seconds	*Minimal rest*
SWITCHKICKS	25 seconds	35 seconds
	Rest 20–30 seconds	*Rest 20 seconds*
	Do 3 rounds	Do 3 rounds
Section 2		
WALKING PLANK	10–12 reps	14–16 reps
	Rest 10–15 seconds	*Minimal rest*
PRONE LAT PULL-DOWNS	12–14 reps	14–16 reps
	Rest 10–15 seconds	*Minimal rest*
SQUAT JACKS	25 seconds	35 seconds
	Rest 20–30 seconds	*Rest 20 seconds*
	Do 3 rounds	Do 3 rounds
Section 3		
STRAIGHT-LEG CRUNCHES	16 reps	18–20 reps
	Rest 10–15 seconds	*Minimal rest*
HEEL TOUCHES	16 reps	18–20 reps
	Rest 10–15 seconds	*Minimal rest*
OBLIQUE CRUNCHES	16 reps	18–20 reps
	Rest 10–15 seconds	*Minimal rest*
LADDER CLIMBS	25 seconds	35 seconds
	Rest 20–30 seconds	*Rest 20 seconds*
	Do 3 rounds	Do 3 rounds

WEEK THREE WORKOUT 3
WHOLE BODY (no cardio)

	NEWBIES 22 minutes	PROS 24 minutes
Section 1		
This is a bit different. You ultimately end up doing all four exercises three times, but you do them by working your way down the list, then up, then back down again! a) SUMO SQUATS b) SQUAT JUMPS c) WALL SQUATS d) WIDE TOE TAPS	Do a), b), c) then d), for 25 seconds each exercise *Rest 15 seconds between each exercise* *Rest 40 seconds when complete* Then go in reverse: d), c), b) and a) for 25 seconds each Then back down: a), b), c) then d) again for 25 seconds each *Rest 1 minute before moving on to Section 2*	Do a), b), c) then d), for 35 seconds each exercise *Rest 15 seconds between each exercise* *Rest 30 seconds when complete* Then go in reverse: d), c), b) and a) for 35 seconds each Then back down: a), b), c) then d) again for 35 seconds each *Rest 1 minute before moving on to Section 2*
Section 2		
a) PULSE PRESS-UPS b) HIGH KNEES c) PRONE LAT PULL-DOWNS d) SWITCHKICKS	Do this section in the same way as Section 1, for the same amount of time	Do this section in the same way as Section 1, for the same amount of time

WEEK THREE WORKOUT 4
WHOLE BODY (with cardio)

	NEWBIES 18 minutes	PROS 22 minutes
Section 1		
This is challenging, but great fun! a) SQUATS WITH SIDE LEG RAISES b) HIP RAISES c) SLOW SQUAT JUMPS d) DEADBUGS e) SQUAT JACKS	Do exercise 1 for 25 seconds *Rest 15 seconds* Then do exercise 1 again, for 25 seconds, immediately followed by exercise 2, rest for 15 seconds. Add exercise 3 to next layer. And so on . . . 1, 1+2, 1+2+3, 1+2+3+4, and finally all 5 exercises *Rest 15 seconds at the end of each layer* *Rest 1 minute before going to Section 2*	Do exercise 1 for 35 seconds *Rest 15 seconds* Then do exercise 1 again, for 35 seconds, immediately followed by exercise 2, rest 15 seconds. Add exercise 3 to next layer. And so on . . . 1, 1+2, 1+2+3, 1+2+3+4, and finally all 5 exercises *Rest 15 seconds at the end of each layer* *Rest 1 minute before going to Section 2*
Section 2		
a) STAR JUMPS b) ABDOMINAL CRUNCHES c) HIGH KNEES d) PRESS-UPS e) SWITCHKICKS	Complete in exactly the same way as Section 1	Complete in exactly the same way as Section 1

ADDITIONAL EXERCISE

'What?! . . . Like extra jumping about? Oh I don't think so.'

Those who take part in the online Blast plan often ask me if they can do other exercise on top of the four Blast workouts each week. (Remember, Blast attracts men and women of all fitness abilities and some have their own exercise firmly entrenched in their routines . . . and nothing will budge them.)

To you and them, I say this: yes, you can add in another workout and you may have a portion of carbohydrates at the following meal, providing that workout has challenged you. For example, if you always go for a jog on Wednesdays with your friend for a catch-up chat, that isn't challenging

(because you can chat) and I would class that as social activity! However, if you can increase the intensity of that catch-up by adding in some spurts of sprinting and some resistance work – like three rounds of 10 squats and 10 press-ups (which means you no longer have the breath to chat) – then, yes, now we're talking. That would be classed as an extra workout.

You should keep in mind that only one portion of starchy carbohydrate per day is the maximum, even if you have done a Blast workout plus something else that is strenuous. You can't have two portions, only one. If you are sticking to just doing the four Blast workouts per week on this plan, then you will have three days without any starchy carbohydrates – which is absolutely fine because you won't go hungry. Promise.

EXERCISE AFTER THE 21 DAYS ARE OVER

In terms of maintaining your Blast way of life after this 21-day plan has finished, I cover all of this in Chapter 12, on both the exercise and nutrition side of things.

You feel different, stronger, fitter and pretty fabulous, inside and out, so it would be tragic for all your efforts to stop on Day 21. We need to find a way of building that effort into your daily life so you can maintain or achieve more. You'll want to learn how to have your cake and eat it. So to speak.

But for the moment, let's head to the next section. Here, I dot the Is and cross the Ts by answering a number of frequently asked questions. There's the chance, too, to see what others have achieved on Blast. Nothing like a gawp at other people's shrinking bodies to galvanise your resolve.

FILLING IN THE GAPS

4

KNOWLEDGE IS POWER

Chapter 10

FREQUENTLY ASKED QUESTIONS

This section is a treat – full of stuff to complete your understanding of successful fat loss and to fire up your willpower and motivation. Your questions are answered, well-known myths are dissected and in Chapter 11 there are 21 day-by-day messages from me to you. These are designed as little 'tell it as it is' doses of motivation for you to read (inhale, even) as you progress through the plan.

Then there's the exciting bit – re-measuring! And, of course, gloating. We also take an in-depth look at life after Blast to help you stride forwards with confidence when the 21 days are over.

Firstly, just so you are quite clear about how to embark on this 21-day adventure, here are some questions most asked by our Blast-ers around the world.

Remind me again, why are carbohydrates restricted?

It's actually only the starchy and sweet stuff that's restricted. Vegetables are still carbohydrates and you can have veritable mountains of those. OK, here's a quick recap. When you eat carbohydrate, it is turned into glucose in the bloodstream. Insulin is produced to pack it off to the right cells to be used. If there's not much demand for it, then insulin sweeps it up and sends it to the fat cells for storage. After the glucose, the body's next preferred fuel is protein (i.e. your muscle), because it takes more effort for the body to empty those fat cells and convert it to stuff it can use. But, on Blast, you're going to be hanging on to your muscle and eating in a way that will release that fat from those fat cells – so it becomes free fatty acids – and that will become your fuel.

Your starchy and sugary carbs will be eaten only after your workout and they will help the body recover and feed the cells that need them. Your muscles will be used in the workouts, and will get firmer and stronger, so the body has no choice but to switch to your fat stores to fuel itself through the day.

Why is fruit limited too?

You can have a portion of low-carbohydrate fruit (blueberries, strawberries, blackcurrants, raspberries, peaches, melon, etc.) at any time. One piece of any other fruit is permitted but only on the days you exercise, as a snack or as dessert.

Remember, we're also working on conquering your sweet tooth, which can scupper even the most disciplined of minds. It's very easy to constantly graze on apples and bananas.

So, in the meal that follows my workout, can I have both a portion of starchy carbohydrates and a piece of fruit?

Yes. For example a sweet potato on your main plate with your protein and your vegetables, and then a piece of fruit as dessert or save it for later on as a snack.

I don't fancy your milk options — almond, hemp, coconut, goat's milk, soya. Won't they taste disgusting?

Actually, they won't. Almond milk in your porridge is surprisingly creamy and goat's milk is just the job in your hot drinks. It's a case of training our taste buds. Try them with an open mind and then take a view on it when the 21 days are done. But you won't know till you try.

What about fizzy drinks? You don't mention those.

Fizzy water is of course fabulous (although between you and me, I never find it as hydrating as still water) but the sweet bubbles of a Cola drink are going to do nothing for you. No, not even the sugar-free ones. Their phosphoric-acid, sodium-citrate or citric-acid content wears away enamel and erodes teeth. Take it from someone who drank two to three cans of Diet Coke every day for about five years, which resulted in two of my back molars crumbling away. Literally. They will also keep your tongue and brain wired up to wanting sweet fulfilment all the time.

I work full time and have a young family. The only time I can fit in the workouts is when I get home in the evening. Shall I do them before dinner? What if I'm so hungry when I get home that I need to eat right then and there, and do the workout when the food has gone down? When will I fit in my starchy carbs portion?

This is a common question. If you can, it's better to do the workout before your meal, but in situations like this we need to adopt a little flexibility. So you can either eat your dinner (with carbs) and then do your workout. Or eat dinner without carbs, do your workout, go to bed and have your post-workout carbs at breakfast. Ideally, you should try to stick to the guidelines set out in Chapter 5, but life doesn't always let us.

Do I absolutely have to do four workouts per week?

Yes. That's why they're there. They're not long and they provide a good mix of strength training and short bursts of cardio.

Can I do extra workouts? To earn extra carbs?

As I explained in Chapter 9, if that workout is a walk round the park with a mate, then by all means do that (and stay in that lovely habit), but on this plan, that does not earn you carbohydrate. If that walk becomes an interval-training walk, where you might do some jogging between trees or some step-ups on benches, then, yes, you earn carbohydrate in the meal that follows. If you do two workouts per day, then you still only get one portion of carbohydrates per day. That's because workouts on your own are never going to be as hard as if I were standing over you. We are also trying to minimise the amount of carbohydrate in order to manage insulin production (which leads to fat storage).

'Just wanted to let you know that I feel amazing. For the first time in years I am sleeping as soon as my head touches the pillow and staying asleep through the night (I'm a long-time sufferer of disturbed sleep). My skin looks amazing, I don't feel bloated or sluggish, my poo is definitely much better, and the big hitter for me is that I can concentrate properly.'

A.L., Nottingham

Do I have to eat the carbs? Won't I lose weight faster if I don't have them? I've heard they're bad.

Yes, you do have to eat them and, no, they're not bad. They will replace the energy used, help your body recover and will fuel you and your muscles throughout the day. No carbs leads to low energy, anxiety, your body feeling weak and downright grumpiness, never mind loss of nutrients.

But . . .

Fingers in ears . . . la la la la la.

And then there's fats – aren't they fattening? Some of the recipes include nuts, avocados, salmon, beef. That makes me nervous.

Listen, if you're really serious about laying the best foundations for a healthy body, inside and out, now and for the future, then I'm telling you straight: your diet has to include fat for making new cells, for the production of hormones, for the absorption of fat-soluble vitamins and for essential fatty acids (which are fats our bodies can't make and which we have to get from our food). If you turn your back on them, then you are neglecting, not nourishing, your body. (Get me, coming over all feisty . . .)

I might be over-stepping the mark here, but is it possible to do the Blast plan by following the food side but by not doing the workouts?

Right, let me put it like this: using your muscles in the workouts makes you stronger and fitter. Yeah, so what, I hear you say. It also means the body will want to use your fat stores for fuel and let your muscle get on with getting firm. The human body would rather hang on to fat – that's how we're made – but if we use the muscle and feed it with protein to keep it strong and toned (rather than weak and wobbly), our fat will be used to keep everything else ticking along.

Apart from the prospect of looking utterly gorgeous, how will I keep motivated throughout the 21 days?

During the online Blast plan (www.theblastplan.com) all the participants follow exactly the same eating plan as described in this book. They also do four workouts a week, just like you, and these are sent to them every week by email. One of the most popular features of the online Blast plan (apart from the results they get!) is the email they receive from me every single day. It's jolly news, health tips, funny stories … anything and everything to keep all of them motivated, entertained and on track.

I have done the same in this book. You've got your guidelines, you've got your understanding and you've got your workouts, all tucked under your arm ready for you to go. So the next chapter contains 21 little messages, a bit like mini letters, to help you through each day.

'Day 8 and I'm wearing a bulldog clip to hold up the trousers I wore a week ago.'

N.H., London

Chapter 11

DAY-BY-DAY MOTIVATION

to keep you groovy, gorgeous and on track throughout the Blast plan

Here are 21 little messages from me to you, which are a taste of the emails I send every single day to those on the online Blast plan. I have a pretty good idea of what's going through your head, which is comforting if your legs ache, your head is thumping and you could murder a doughnut.

DAY 1

So you've started! Brilliant. Let's grab this fat-loss and fitness adventure by the scruff and give it our best. You're organised with your meal planning and you've got your lunch boxes ready to fill to the brim with goodies so that you're not tempted by the office cakes (because we KNOW how they're going to sabotage our fat-loss plans and make us nod off in the afternoon). Get your food and mood diary started with entry number one: 'Day 1 – Feeling excited and positive.' Remember to keep your social calendar going – this isn't about being lonesome with a bowl of lettuce. It's about enjoying lots of lovely food but saying no thanks to the wine. And feeling terribly self-satisfied.

DAY 2

'I feel a bit strange, different, sort of "not with it".'

Yes, you might have a headache, a spaced-out feeling, maybe even a funny taste in your mouth. It's working. Hurrah! The worse your diet was before in terms of sugar, processed foods and caffeine, the worse you may feel. Aim for a positive frame of mind. Think along the lines of, My halo is dazzling, rather than, I want to kill someone now . . . right now.

DAY 3

I expect you've done a workout by now. Did you give it everything? If it left parts of you groaning and gasping, then we've done our job. If not, then a bit more depth in those squats and a bit more speed in those mountain climbers and you'll have cracked it. Everyone's fitness level is different, but so is their mindset . . . and pain threshold. The headache may still be lingering, and that's normal. Soothe yourself by spouting a few facts about insulin and carbs to your work colleagues or family just as they're tucking into their crisps and afternoon chocolate.

DAY 4

It's about now that the fog might start to clear. Hallelujah. As one Blast member said, 'I look upon it as a holiday for my body, a rest, a retreat. It's the bad stuff leaving my body to make room for the good stuff.' You might still be feeling that your retreat is more a wet weekend's camping than a sun-drenched orange grove, but we're only on Day 4. Your body is still preparing itself for change. Let it.

DAY 5

I bet you jumped out of bed with gusto this morning. You feel different, like everything is speeding up inside. You've cracked the first few days and now *nothing* is going to stop you. The desire to harm any living thing that so much as looks at you has disappeared and it seems that something resembling sanity has been restored.

DAY 6

Beaten anyone with the broccoli stick today? If not, go and bore your friends and family with the antioxidant routine. Remember to pile those vegetables high (we LOVE volume) and feel your body sizzling with delight as all those vits and mins strut their stuff in your bloodstream. It's another step towards better health and skin and (just as important) another notch up on the smug-o-meter.

DAY 7

You're really in the groove now. You're ticking your boxes:

Workout: done

Carbs: eaten (devoured!)

Cake: ignored (although you did have to sniff it)

Trousers: looser

Self-esteem: rocking

You've nailed a marvellous routine of workouts and food, and you're not missing the piles of bread one bit. You've still got some friends, you're not divorced (yet) and the whole family seems to be tucking into their meals with something approaching bold enthusiasm. This is good; this is getting really good.

DAY 8

You've done a week, woo hoo! . . . and you're surprised (delighted, even) to realise that you're spending less time thinking about food. You don't seem to be hungry in between meals, you can turn a blind eye to the office biccies, and words like 'positive mindset', 'energy' and 'squats' are becoming part of your daily vocabulary. You're standing your ground and you really quite like it.

DAY 9

The scales are looking at you, waving at you.

'Cooo-eeee, over here. Go on, get on, no one's to know!'

But you want to do it right and you resist because you know weight isn't an indicator of success. Instead you shut the bedroom door and give the mirror the full-frontal treatment. Wow. Your stomach has gone down, your thighs and arms are losing their slackness and your face has taken on an almost chiselled look. There's a spring in your step, a glow to your cheeks and a pertness to your bottom . . . must be all that walking to the toilet.

'I'm now a week into the Blast plan and I'm noticing some amazing things. I have never felt so in control around food in a natural, unforced way. I am not hungry in between meals, I don't bother snacking and I am really enjoying my food. I have definitely lost weight, judging by my trousers, and feel immensely calm.'

J.C., Edinburgh

DAY 10

Oh. There's a potential setback looming large. An invitation to a friend's birthday. It's on Saturday night (therefore expectations for total liver annihilation are high) and the food will be all your faves. Think carbs overload. There's only one thing for it: bare-faced lies: 'Actually I'm on really strong antibiotics, which make me feel nauseous …' Maybe even go one step further and say you have a bit of an gynae thing going on and do the whole pointing 'down below' routine. No one will ever ask again.

DAY 11

So, you're doing well with your workouts; that's great to hear. You're past the halfway point now, so do make sure that you're still putting everything you can into them. Remember, fat loss is not about doing cardio all the time. The strength work is there in the Blast plan for a reason. To tone, hone and increase your testosterone levels. To lower stress levels (and blood pressure), raise self-esteem and improve your strength.

I'm making it sound so simple, aren't I? Turn a blind eye to cake, eat your greens, do your squats and feel like hugging someone. Basically, it IS that simple.

DAY 12

So let's just have a recap about food. To remind yourself of the rules, flick back to pages 54–5 just in case you've been tempted to let things slide a little. You haven't felt bloated, your ankles aren't puffy, your eczema has gone down and your poo (ahem) is a wonderful rich brown.

You might think your body is crying out for carbs. But is it? Is it really? Are you sure it's not your emotions getting in the way? There will be days when you're not exercising (and therefore not having your portion of starchy carbs), so just plan your meals to the last detail to avoid getting caught short in front of a sweet shop with a Chunky KitKat staring you in the face.

DAY 13

People are really starting to notice now. Your skin is different, smoother even, and nothing feels tight any more. Your bottom has a delicious ache about it (those squat jumps are a menace) and you've found yourself starting to walk that little bit taller. Let's not pretend, though … you're gagging for a slice of Colin from Accounts' leaving cake and you're still twitchy every time someone mentions the pub, but so far you haven't caved in. And you feel so jolly proud of yourself.

DAY 14

Here is the point where you might be thinking, Only another seven days to go. Yes, only another seven days on Blast, but what then? So this is where you read, inhale, worship and, if the neighbours are a tolerant bunch, chant the Blast guidelines (see pages 54–5). Remember these 21 days are pretty strict, but no one is asking you to relinquish your favourite food and drink for ever. Never have it again. Be no fun. Lose all your friends. Join a nunnery. No, of course not. But Day 14 is not cave-in day, OK? It's the day when you realise you have done without those habits for fourteen days! Those habits that have possibly been preventing you from getting into shape for years. And are you going to go back and undo all that? Not if I have anything to do with it.

DAY 15

So in your workouts, which are getting progressively harder now (had you noticed?!), let's get a cracking pace on. Let's really beat the stuffing out of some fat cells. I'm not saying do them at a mad pace, I'm saying let's get your technique spot on. Super-low squats, lunges and press-ups. Work safely but well. Try not to miss anything out, just because you're not 'feeling the love' that day. Just bite it off, chew it and spit it out, as my Dad used to say (about my chemistry homework). You will be so chuffed with yourself.

DAY 16

Today may have been a fabulous day. It may also have been a shockingly terrible day. It started to rain, the trains were up the creek, you were late for work, your Blast lunch is still in the fridge (at home), your feet hurt, your period is due so your skirt is tight and you feel fat, frayed and fractious. Your boss found fault, your daughter found love and your friend found a bottle of wine that she's bringing round tonight and you're frightened you might give in. It's the last straw.

None of it will be Blast's fault. None of it is anyone's fault. It's just life. But you're strong and it takes more than that lot to make you crumble.

DAY 17

You've realised all of a sudden how calm you've been over these past few days. How chilled. And that's because you know this way of eating and exercise suits you, and that it works. So you're not letting your guard down anytime soon.

You've got your Blast tools under your arm and you're ready to fly out into the world as a fully fledged Blast graduate. Spread those wings and soar into the face of anyone who says you can't keep this going.

'Oh for goodness' sake, Annie, I'm not interested in your poetry. I want pats on the back, fists punching the air, cheers, shouts and raucous encouragement.'

It's coming, lovely people.

DAY 18

Hot news. You've just tried on that dress again. Oh yes, yes, yes! Those buttons do up a dream. That's perfect, just as we want it, because soon (on Day 22) you will need to re-do your measurements. No, don't be nervous, it's the fun bit. Your reward. And it's why you're doing this. To see results, face up to new habits and feel a sense of achievement.

DAY 19

You're feeling really quite perky, and you've secretly confessed to yourself that you quite like this Blast malarkey and you don't want any of it to end. You like the carb control and the feeling of being set free from sugar dependence, never mind the deep sleep and the short, sharp workouts. Yeah, OK, you can't deny a little glass of wine wouldn't go amiss, but you're strong now and so you can resist.

DAY 20

Today is a good day to think about new goals. Look at the ones you set yourself when you started Blast and decide what's next. Maybe one or more of the following:

- To replace most of my clothes with new ones, two sizes smaller

- To continue to exercise three or four times a week but not let it rule my life

- To lose another inch off my hips

- To enjoy food and wine but not use it as a crutch

- To feel proud of myself

DAY 21

A day for feeling proud. And pretty jolly gorgeous. Keep on track today because tomorrow is results day. If you have a workout planned for today, then do it. And do it with bells on. Look back over your food and mood diary and laugh at your jottings of 'stinking headache' and how you could 'kill for a Snickers bar'. Come on . . . there's a plan to be made.

THE DAY AFTER . . .

Dig out your numbers sheet and re-measure all those places you measured 21 days ago. Write down those smaller numbers and do a little dance. Then store those results carefully. Next, strip off and re-take your photos. All angles! If you're planning on weighing yourself again, only do so if it's not going to play with your mind. Best policy is to think something like, I may have lost one pound but I don't care because it's not important.

Because it isn't! Remember, we're not aiming for lighter. We're aiming for smaller, trimmer, healthier.

Now is the time to think to yourself how you are going to take this Blast plan forward but still get results. You've spent 21 days undergoing massive changes in your eating and in your routine. You stuck to it. Who says you can't continue that way? With a few deviations maybe.

Not only will your results be evident on the outside, you will have undoubtedly felt better on the inside, too. No one knows your body like you do, so it will be only you who decides what you can cope with. Can you give up wheat for ever? Did you miss it? And what about alcohol and animal dairy? Can you adjust them to being 'occasional' deviations? Everyone has different lifestyles and different situations at home, but it's up to you, and only you, to make permanent changes, if YOU want to.

You have developed a wonderful sense of focus and discipline over the last 21 days. If you can keep just some of that and make it a permanent feature of your daily life, then you're on to a winner. Be careful of social media and try not to compare yourself to how someone half your age might look. They may not have houses, partners, children, companies to run and long commutes.

Let's take a look at how we can adapt the stringent guidelines of Blast to everyday life.

Chapter 12

ADAPTING BLAST TO EVERYDAY LIFE

'I feel very pleased with myself. Sticking to eating plans has defeated me for a long time. Usually by the end of Day 2, I have thrown in the towel and opened a packet of crisps. This is a revelation.'

J.F., London

So much has been achieved! You've realised that over the past 21 days, you've not only kicked some bad habits, but you've adopted some new ones, too. You've lost inches, gained confidence as well as fitness and you have some calm back in your gut as well as in your mind and mood. You have energy, vigour and sparkle. The daily bloat has gone and the glow has returned in your demeanour as well as your cheeks. You can hardly recognise this person. You've swapped bread for broccoli, sweets for sweating, and lethargy for lunges.

So, what now?

Well, you can do one of three things:

Number 1: You can either tick the Blast box, dump your trainers (and this book) in the bin and heave a sigh of relief:

'Thank goodness that's over . . . if I never see another green vegetable or do another squat it will be far too soon.'

You can then take up the reins of your old life with a 'now, where were we?' approach.

Number 2: You can continue with your workouts and with the Blast plan guidelines, changing nothing at all. You may find that never, ever having alcohol has done you a massive favour and you'd like to continue exactly as you have been over the past 21 days.

Number 3: This third option seems to be the most popular with our online Blast customers around the world – and that is sticking to the Blast guidelines but with a little more flexibility. Small tweaks, like adding in a little bread and pasta now and then and a nibble of chocolate, will mean you will continue to get consistent results because it feels more doable (which is code for your sanity being saved). Keep a close eye on how your gut feels and make notes of how it copes with the reintroduction of some foods. Be careful not to sink back into old ways; so keep tabs on your body measurements too and how you feel in your clothes.

Let's take a closer look at how Blast can be adapted long term.

FOOD

1. **Carbohydrate consumption:** Keep the starchy carbs to once a day, and, yes, even at the weekends. Aim to have them in the meal that follows a workout, but if this becomes too restrictive, then have your one portion at a time convenient to you. But do aim to have at least two carb-free days per week.

2. **Protein:** If it's not on your plate at every meal time, get twitchy and do something about it. Meat, fish, beans, tofu, pulses, protein powder, a little cheese, yoghurt, seafood . . . make sure it's there in front of you. This will keep you full, ensure insulin levels remain stable and feed your muscles – which you're obviously still going to be using.

3. **Wheat:** If you have missed sinking your teeth into a doorstep of bread, and you feel no ill effects from eating wheat, then have a slice or two as your carb portion a couple of times a week. Make careful notes about how your body reacts. Choose a good homemade variety and stay away from the spongy stuff in a plastic wrapper. Spelt and sourdough are good choices to minimise digestive upheaval. The same goes for pasta – some just cannot imagine life permanently without it.

4. **Dairy:** If you haven't felt the love for the dairy alternatives, then reintroduce dairy a little at a time. Try goat's milk as this is much gentler on the gut than cow's. Add some goat and sheep's cheese to your meals a couple of times a week (two or three thin slices of chèvre tucked inside your breakfast omelette is delicious). Keep the high-protein yoghurt going, too, as it's an easy way to maintain high protein levels, and it lends itself to every meal.

5. **Caffeine:** You may find that post-Blast your adherence to this rule starts to slide a little. You can't deny how great you felt (after the colossal headache had passed) once you'd kicked the four lattes habit and dropped to one a day, so do try and aim to keep cortisol and insulin in check by maintaining the one caffeinated drink per day rule.

6. **Fluid:** Just 3 litres per day. No messin'. Besides, you still have endless boxes of herbal tea to wade through (never mind the endless trips to the toilet).

7. **Alcohol:**

   'Uh, oh. What's she going to say?'

   I don't think it's going to be a surprise. It does us no favours in the fat-loss game, does it? (See page 44 for a reminder.) Make a plan of how little you and your lifestyle can get away with during the week – this will minimise the damage done by those times when impromptu social gatherings get the better of you.

8. **Portion sizes:** You've hopefully spent the last 21 days paying much more attention to the quantity of food on your plate. Keep that habit up, but there's no need to become obsessed – just being gently mindful is perfect. On non-carb days, remember to fill gaps on your plate with vegetables and some pulses or beans. Spread the veggie love in

your family to encourage a more balanced approach to food. There doesn't always have to be a space for potato.

9. Deviations: Celebrations, anniversaries, holidays and the odd Friday night of gay abandon (when a glass becomes a bottle) are bound to happen. This is part of life and they are to be enjoyed. But try not to blow the whole week based on one deviation. Make the most of the occasion and then get back in the Blast saddle and crack on. Feel no guilt, just empowerment.

10. Cakes, pastries, chocolate: The things you haven't had for 21 days . . . I find a good policy is this: decide what you really, really like, then plan them as an occasional treat. Have you avoided having brunch with a friend each week because it always used to involve extra-large croissants and piles of jam? Then keep that appointment but switch to eggs and avocado on a piece of posh artisan toast, or have the croissants but sneak in an extra mini-workout. It is more often the sugary foods that send our brain (and our hormones) a bit bonkers and then it has trouble deciding if we're full or not. So it encourages us then to eat more of them, 'just to be on the safe side'. Don't fall into that trap. There is so much more in life that demands our attention and we don't want to spend time fighting our own conscience. You've done Blast and it worked as a whole package. There may be bits of it you can drop (it won't be the exercise, sorry to dash your hopes) and still get results, still feel in control, still feel energetic and gorgeous. Now on to post-Blast exercise.

EXERCISE

So here's where I get serious. It doesn't come naturally, but I'll give it my best shot.

Exercise isn't just for the 21 days. It's not something I've added to make the whole Blast adventure more revolting and hateful – like cough mixture, the worse it tastes the more good it must be doing. For you to stay in shape, maintain your renewed energy level and continue to lose fat (coupled with your Blast eating principles), keeping that exercise habit is vital. Challenging your muscles is vital.

In this book you were prescribed four workouts per week (see Chapter 9), which were progressive throughout the 21 days. They are a mix, as you found out, of a) strength work, which makes your muscles firmer and stronger (and which demand more energy to keep them like that), and b) short, sharp, cardio work, which builds endurance, develops fitness, burns fat and boosts your metabolism.

So when you've completed the 21 Day Blast plan, you can either repeat all three weeks' workouts again – this time adding on five or so extra reps in the strength sections – or for even more motivation and variety, you can log on, for free, to my YouTube channel (www.youtube.com/anniedeadman/). There you'll find masses of workouts to do at home – all 15–30 minutes long, both beginner and advanced. You just pick one, click and off you go.

These video workouts feature my colleague Aaron Roberts (he runs the personal training side of the business) and me. He's telling me and you what to do and pushing us through it. He looks smart, the instruction is clear and the teaching points are spot on. Then there's me. Sweating, puffing, moaning, hair in a mess . . . it's really not pretty, but I'm doing the whole workout with you. A kind of partner in crime, so all you have to do is get your trainers on and we can hate him together . . .

These workouts are anything but dull. There's plenty of laughter (mostly at my expense), but we work hard, which means you will be motivated enough to do the same. They're effective, easily squeezable into your day and they're fun.

Home workouts are a brilliant way of fitting challenging exercise into your day without having to trek out to the local gym – especially if you are at the mercy of time constraints or small children. Block the time out in your diary and make it part of your weekly routine. You can increase the effects of some of the moves by doing extra reps, reducing your rest time, or adding in dumbbells. Be true to yourself, though – the tendency to dodge the discomfort of squat jumps and opt for low-level star jumps is all too tempting!

If you get sick of us (it happens), you can make up your own home workouts, but just make sure there is a good balance of high-intensity cardio (short bursts, thankfully) and some good, slow strength work, taking your muscles out of their comfort zone.

Whatever you choose as your exercise option, it should overload your muscles so that they have to adapt by becoming firmer and stronger. It should also be doable for you and, dare I say it, enjoyable.

No one knows what's round the corner, no one at all.

'Oh no. She's going maudlin on us . . .'

Well, we don't, do we? What we do know is that body has got to get you through the rest of your life, so let's nourish and cherish it and give yourself the best chance of maintaining your health and energy. It's also about confidence and contentment; nothing ravages a woman's psyche more than her disgruntlement at how she looks and feels.

Blast is such a simple plan, with small demands on your time, but the promises are big and the results and benefits are huge.

So tuck this Blast bible somewhere safe and let's crack on. We have work to do.

THE END

Annie Deadman's online Blast plans run regularly throughout the year. These amount to 21 days of fat loss, recalibration, effective workouts, laughter and a way of eating that will soothe your head and your gut.

Websites: www.anniedeadman.com and www.theblastplan.com

Facebook: www.facebook.com/anniedeadmantraining/

Instagram: www.instagram.com/anniedeadman/

Youtube: www.youtube.com/anniedeadman/

'I was amazed, staggered even, at what I achieved and learnt in those 21 days. So much of Blast has become everyday for me now. I just don't want to go back to how I was.'

G.B., Bristol (7 inches)

'Just wanted to let you know that I am now wearing a vest without the back fat scenario. Hurrah!'

R.M., London

'Frankly for me, this is the Holy Grail.'

J.B., London

'The total loss is 12½ inches! I don't know what I weigh and I no longer care. I just want to look better in my clothes and feel better in myself, so thank you for teaching me that.'

S.B., Surrey

INDEX

ACKNOWLEDGEMENTS

Top of the list I'd like to thank every single person who has been a customer of Blast and of Annie Deadman Training over the past years. YOU are what gets me out of bed every day, and it's you who have helped me develop, improve and expand every aspect of my work. I'd also like to thank Aaron Roberts, my colleague and partner in crime, whose patience I have challenged more than once and whose support has been instrumental in the development of the company. To the wonderful admin team headed up by Stacey, thank you for all you do, providing a sense of calm on my headless-chicken days. To my ex-husband Ade, thank you for saying all the right things, never judging me and coming up with perfect designs every time. To my kindest, most loyal friend Tiphanie, whose cottage I hid away in to write, whose support was limitless but who always gave me the truth, never a load of flannel. May we continue to guffaw with laughter. Hugs and kisses to my two daughters, Emily and Sara, whose encouragement, reassurance and tell-it-like-it-is approach never left me in any doubt that I could do it. So lovely to have you by my side.

Thank you to all my friends, family, bootcampers and work colleagues for keeping this under wraps and for letting me ramble on. Special thanks to those of you who lured me away from the laptop to go for walks and to tread thousands of steps up hills and round parks in order that I may offload. Thank you for nodding in the right places.

A special thank you (oh, go on then . . . a glass of fizz) to the broadcaster, author and comedian Viv Groskop, whose shouting about Blast from the rooftops helped get us national press coverage. Yes, this is all your fault!

Lastly, thanks to the nutritionist Joy Skipper, for help and inspiration in creating such a collection of delicious recipes. And to the teams at Curtis Brown and at HarperCollins for a) taking part in the Blast plan, and really rather loving it, and b) believing it was worth putting between the covers of a book. Oh, and c) coping with my endless questions.

Thank you, everyone,

Annie x

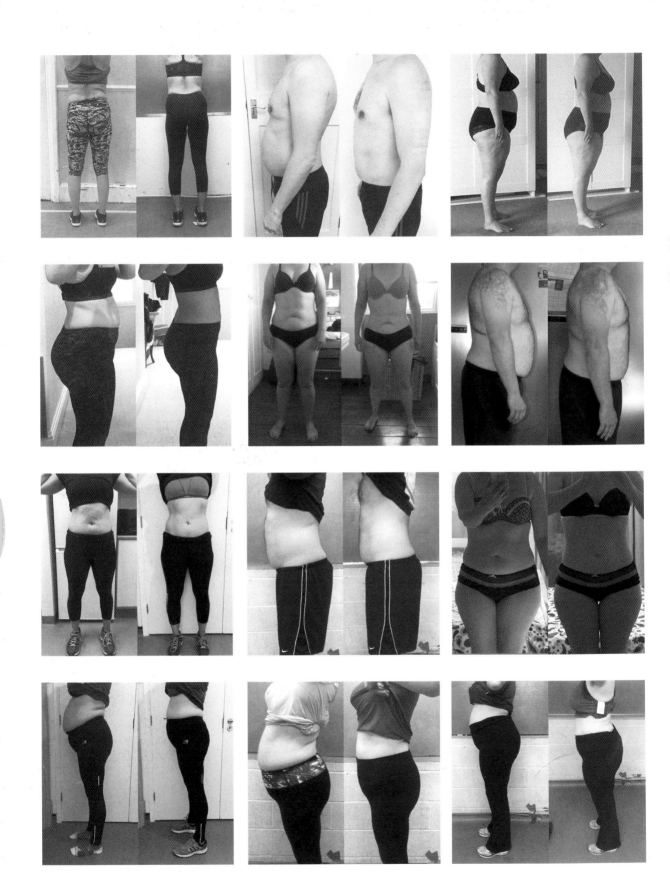